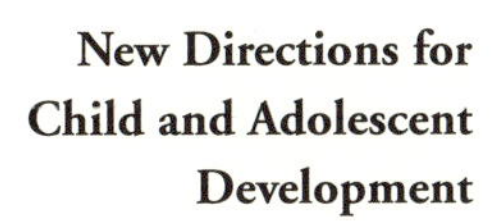
New Directions for Child and Adolescent Development

Children's Moral Emotions and Moral Cognition:
Developmental and Educational Perspectives

Brigitte Latzko
Tina Malti
EDITORS

Number 129 • Fall 2010
Jossey-Bass
San Francisco

Children's Moral Emotions and Moral Cognition: Developmental and Educational Perspectives
Brigitte Latzko, Tina Malti (eds.)
New Directions for Child and Adolescent Development, no. 129
Lene Arnett Jensen, Reed W. Larson, Editors-in-Chief

Microfilm copies of issues and articles are available in 16mm and 35mm, as well as microfiche in 105mm, through University Microfilms, Inc., 300 North Zeeb Road, Ann Arbor, Michigan 48106-1346.

ISSN 1520-3247 electronic ISSN 1534-8687

New Directions for Child and Adolescent Development is part of The Jossey-Bass Education Series and is published quarterly by Wiley Subscription Services, Inc., a Wiley company, at Jossey-Bass, 989 Market Street, San Francisco, California 94103-1741. Periodicals postage paid at San Francisco, California, and at additional mailing offices. Postmaster: Send address changes to New Directions for Child and Adolescent Development, Jossey-Bass, 989 Market Street, San Francisco, CA 94103-1741.

New Directions for Child and Adolescent Development is indexed in Cambridge Scientific Abstracts (CSA/CIG), CHID: Combined Health Information Database (NIH), Contents Pages in Education (T&F), Current Abstracts (EBSCO), Educational Research Abstracts Online (T&F), EMBASE/Excerpta Medica (Elsevier), ERIC Database (Education Resources Information Center), Index Medicus/MEDLINE/PubMed (NLM), Linguistics & Language Behavior Abstracts (CSA/CIG), Psychological Abstracts/PsycINFO (APA), Social Services Abstracts (CSA/CIG), SocINDEX (EBSCO), and Sociological Abstracts (CSA/CIG).

Subscription rates: For the U.S., $89 for individuals and $315 for institutions. Please see ordering information page at end of journal.

Editorial correspondence should be e-mailed to the editors-in-chief: Lene Arnett Jensen (ljensen@clarku.edu) and Reed W. Larson (larsonr@illinois.edu).

Jossey-Bass Web address: www.josseybass.com

CONTENTS

Malti, T., & Latzko, B. (2010). Children's moral emotions and moral cognition: Towards an integrative perspective. In B. Latzko & T. Malti (Eds.), *Children's moral emotions and moral cognition: Developmental and educational perspectives. New Directions for Child and Adolescent Development, 129,* 1–10. San Francisco: Jossey-Bass.

1

Children's Moral Emotions and Moral Cognition: Towards an Integrative Perspective

Tina Malti, Brigitte Latzko

Abstract

This chapter presents a brief introduction to the developmental and educational literature linking children's moral emotions to cognitive moral development. A central premise of the chapter is that an integrative developmental perspective on moral emotions and moral cognition provides an important conceptual framework for understanding children's emerging morality and designing developmentally sensitive moral intervention strategies. The subsequent chapters present promising conceptual approaches and empirical evidence linking children's moral emotions to moral cognition. Examples of integrated educational interventions intended to enhance children's moral development are presented and discussed. © Wiley Periodicals, Inc.

View this article online at wileyonlinelibrary.com. • DOI: 10.1002/cd.272

In recent years, the centuries-old debate on how to frame the role of moral emotions and moral cognition in human morality has experienced a renaissance (Malti, Gummerum, & Keller, 2008). Although the issue is far from resolved, there is a consensus that ordinary moral concepts and moral emotions are linked. For example, moral emotions, such as compassion or guilt feelings, are recognized as influencing a person's understanding of the prescriptive nature of the norms of fairness and caring (Nussbaum, 2001). Therefore, developmental researchers have recently called for an integrative approach to the study of moral cognition and moral emotions, as well as their emergence in human development (Smetana & Killen, 2008; Turiel, in press). Although moral judgments are assumed to be at the core of children's morality, it is also claimed that moral emotions help children anticipate the outcomes of sociomoral events and adjust their moral behavior accordingly (Arsenio, Gold, & Adams, 2006). Moral emotions such as sympathy represent a genuine orientation towards the other's welfare; conjointly with moral cognition, they are very important to the early development of moral action tendencies (Eisenberg, 2000; Hoffman, 2000; Keller, 1996; Tangney, Stuewig, & Mashek, 2007).

The emphasis placed on moral emotions in the study of moral cognition and moral behavior has been highlighted in recent theoretical and empirical work, and promising first steps towards empirical integration have been taken. So far, however, the research has not been well integrated, and the few published studies have focused primarily on a particular moral emotion, such as guilt feelings, and its relation to moral cognition. This focus is overly narrow and fails to take account of the role of other moral emotions (e.g., empathy, shame, pride) and moral cognition, as each of these emotions may follow a distinct developmental trajectory. How can we describe these conceptual distinctions, and how can they contribute to the integration of educational efforts aimed at bridging the gap between moral emotions and moral cognition?

In this volume, we conceptualize moral emotions as self-conscious or self-evaluative emotions because the individual's understanding and evaluation of the self are fundamental to emotions such as guilt feelings (Eisenberg, 2000). This description also indicates that cognitive moral processes are closely related to these emotions, and a strict distinction between cognition and emotions seems therefore not necessary (Krettenauer, Malti, & Sokol, 2008). Psychological theories on morality have described emotions such as guilt, empathy, shame, but also positively charged emotions such as pride as a quintessential part of children's emerging morality because these emotions genuinely express a moral orientation of caring and internalized norm orientation; furthermore, they can serve as motives in the genesis of moral action tendencies (Keller, 1996, 2004; Malti & Keller, 2010; Tangney et al., 2007). Without the anticipation of moral emotions, on the other hand, moral knowledge and cognitive moral complexity may be used strategically to achieve personal goals (Gasser & Keller, 2009).

This volume aims to shed light on this debate by discussing how the role of moral emotions and moral cognition in children's emerging morality can best be understood. Examples of educational interventions that integrate moral emotions and moral cognition are also provided.

Developmental Research on Children's Moral Emotions and Moral Cognition

Children increasingly come to understand and make moral judgments in situations involving moral transgressions, as well as anticipate the emotions of the people involved in the situations. But how do moral emotions and moral cognition evolve during the course of childhood and adolescence, and how does their interdependency change across development? These questions are at the heart of developmental research on children's moral emotions and moral cognition. Children experience a variety of emotions during moral conflicts, and these affective representations influence their subsequent judgments and behavior (Arsenio, 2008; Gummerum, Hanoch, & Keller, 2008).

Moral emotions are considered to be self-conscious because they presuppose an understanding of the relation between the self and others that is obtained through self-evaluation (Eisenberg, 2000). In other words, the anticipation of these emotions presupposes the cognitive ability to take the other's perspective (Harris, 1989) and thus shows that moral emotions and moral cognition are interdependent.

Social domain research has shown that young children construct moral judgments from early on and distinguish them from social conventions (Turiel, 1983). Developmental researchers assume that the process of constructing moral judgments in early childhood is likely to be related to the development of empathy and other moral emotions (Helwig, 2008). It is very likely that young children are able to construct moral judgments because they experience situations involving moral transgressions as emotionally salient and they associate moral emotions such as empathy or guilt with these transgressions. It is likely that as children increase their moral understanding, they come to recognize that moral transgressions are serious, generally wrong, and deserving of punishment. This increasing cognitive understanding is most likely associated with more frequent anticipations of moral emotions.

Research in the happy victimizer paradigm has shown that this cognitive moral understanding does not necessarily reflect emotional salience, particularly in young children (for reviews, see Arsenio et al., 2006; Krettenauer et al., 2008). Happy victimizer research has documented that even though young children understand the validity of a moral rule that was violated, they expect the moral wrongdoer to be happy because they focus exclusively on the wrongdoer's personal gain. It is not typical for children under the age of six or seven years to associate moral emotions such as sadness, guilt, or remorse with immoral conduct.

It remains to be seen why children's cognitive moral understanding does not match the corresponding affective reactions, even though moral cognition and moral emotions are interdependent and continuously interact during development. Research on the early precursors of morality provides some interesting insights on this question by showing how early socialization in the family influences the development of a conscience in very young children (Kochanska, Padavich, & Koenig, 1996). However, developmental research explicitly linking moral emotions to moral cognition in childhood is relatively rare and has focused almost exclusively on either the relation between empathy/sympathy and moral cognition, or the association between guilt feelings, as attributed in the happy victimizer paradigm, and moral cognition. For example, studies by Eisenberg and colleagues have shown that sympathy is related to children's altruistic moral reasoning and that these two variables conjointly predict prosocial behavior (see Eisenberg, Spinrad, & Sadovsky, 2006, for a review). The few studies that have directly addressed the relationship of emotions such as guilt to moral cognition have yielded inconsistent results. For example, Smetana, Campione-Barr, and Yell (2003) found few associations between the emotions attributed to a perpetrator and moral judgments by six- to eight-year-old children. In contrast, a recent study by Malti, Gasser, and Gutzwiller-Helfenfinger (2010) documented that the moral reasoning of five- to nine-year-old children was negatively related to their attributions of happy feelings and positively related to their attributions of guilt feelings.

In conclusion, although developmental studies have supported the view that moral emotions play an important role in determining how children deal with moral conflict situations, and that these moral emotions relate to cognitive moral understanding in meaningful ways, relatively few studies have investigated the relation between various moral emotions and moral cognition in the course of development. We also lack a systematic developmental approach to the study of children's emerging moral emotions and moral cognition. This astonishing state should stimulate efforts to clarify the role of both factors in the development of a child's morality and the complexity inherent in this process (Arsenio et al., 2006). Specifically, it remains unclear what are (a) the developmental relations between moral emotions and cognition, and (b) the varying relations among different types of moral emotions (e.g., sympathy, guilt, pride) and moral cognition.

Developing Children's Moral Emotions and Moral Cognition through Education

Despite the increasing consensus among developmental researchers that moral emotions and moral cognition are interdependent and reciprocally interact with each other over the course of development, most of the common moral interventions in childhood have focused on promoting children's cognitive moral development. This focus seems surprising, as current developmental research indicates rather consistently that although children understand the validity of moral rules, they do not necessarily understand the emotional consequences of following or breaking them. As immoral conduct is, in part, related to this lack of moral emotions, it is important to introduce a wide range of moral emotions into educational practice in a systematic way. The failure so far to do so is also surprising because moral emotions such as guilt or sympathy have been shown to relate to prosocial dispositions (Eisenberg et al., 2006; Malti, Gummerum, Keller, & Buchmann, 2009), and these dispositions are a key goal of many social-emotional learning programs. In short, educational research appears to lag behind developmental research in the process of integrating children's moral cognition and moral emotions.

This strong emphasis on the promotion of cognitive moral growth can be traced back to the Kohlbergian tradition. One of the best-known educational approaches to enhancing cognitive moral development is the Just Community, an approach in the Kohlberg tradition. This approach, which has been widely and successfully applied (Kohlberg, 1984; see Oser, Althof, & Higgins-D'Alessandro, 2008), focuses on the promotion of competence in moral judgments by stimulating the development of cognitive structures through moral dialogue, moral interactions, and participation. One can assume that interaction and participation are also important resources for teaching moral emotions. In the Just Community approach, learning of moral emotions may tend to be spontaneous rather than explicit or systematic. However, the teaching of moral emotions is not mentioned as such in the presentations of the Just Community's theoretical framework. A strategy commonly used in the Just Community classroom to promote cognitive moral growth is the dilemma discussion. This technique has become popular because its effectiveness in enhancing the competence of moral judgments has been validated by research and can easily be adapted to many school subjects (see Lind, 2010; Patry, Weyringer, & Weinberger, 2007).

Moral reasoning and judgment skills are only one dimension of morality, however. It remains necessary to adapt the goals and purposes of moral education to the demands of a multicultural, pluralistic society, including a person's morality (Buxarraias, Martínez, Noguera, & Tey, 2003). Researchers have therefore emphasized the need to include the inculcation of moral emotions and moral action in efforts to develop moral competence (Latzko, 2008, 2010). Such an integrative educational approach is the most likely to develop responsible and caring future generations in democratic societies (Edelstein, 2010).

To date, there is no educational approach that explicitly addresses the promotion of moral emotions in childhood (see *Handbook of Moral and*

Character Education, Nucci & Narvaez, 2008). Although the *Handbook of Moral Development* has described promising conceptual approaches to the study of children's moral emotions (Killen & Smetana, 2006), the educational implications of these insights appear to be in its infancy. Interventions aimed at promoting moral emotions occur predominantly in formal social-emotional learning programs, as well as in violence prevention programs such as Second Step. However, these programs tend to focus almost exclusively on the promotion of empathy. Moreover, it is common for only the cognitive component of empathy to be considered, or else the program does not distinguish between the cognitive and affective components of empathy. Finally, only a handful of intervention approaches distinguish between the various moral emotions and systematically enhance these individual components of children's morality.

In this volume, we discuss the educational approaches that overcome this problem and integrate the developmental models of moral emotion and cognition. These efforts have the potential to facilitate children's ethical development holistically and are thus a promising vehicle for enhancing their cognitive and affective moral growth (Nucci & Narvaez, 2008). The emphasis that these approaches place on the need to integrate different moral emotions in moral education is grounded in the fact that the feelings children experience in everyday moral situations have consequences for both the self and others; thus, they are important for the continued development of cognitive and affective decentration (Latzko, 2008). Emotional experiences in real-life situations can be meaningfully used as a basis for, and play a key role in initiating, children's moral learning. It is therefore important to raise educators' awareness of real-life moral conflict situations as a resource for moral education. By studying specific conflict situations and the emotions they invoke in the child—as victim, perpetrator, bystander, and/or observer—the teacher can help inculcate sociomoral sensitivity. Thus, sensitizing educators to the variety of interventions they can use in specific situations, as well as the emotions that these interventions can elicit, are key to stimulating moral growth. The present volume illustrates this proposition qualitatively using case studies.

Overview of the Volume

This volume discusses how moral emotions and moral cognition contribute to children's morality by focusing on the developmental relations between children's various moral emotions and moral cognition in different methodological contexts. This examination expresses the central theme of the volume, namely, how integrating moral emotions and moral cognition can help us understand the development of children's morality. Furthermore, the volume addresses several implications of this knowledge for education. Each chapter considers the relationships between moral emotions and moral cognition from both the developmental and educational perspectives.

The second chapter, by Eveline Gutzwiller-Helfenfinger, Luciano Gasser, and Tina Malti, moves beyond hypothetical moral issues and presents empirical findings on children's responses to real-life transgressions and their conversations about the everyday conflicts they experience. They compare the naturally occurring moral judgments and emotions of kindergarten and elementary school children, as expressed in spontaneously generated narratives about interpersonal moral conflicts, with those in hypothetical situations. In the real-life cases, children attribute a variety of various negative emotions such as anger, guilt, sadness, and fear to themselves as perpetrators, and these emotions and judgments differ from those that are evoked by hypothetical transgressions.

In the third chapter, Bruce Maxwell and Sarah DesRoches critically discuss the use of empathy in formal social-emotional learning programs. The authors highlight three common pitfalls of empathy use in typical programs of this type. First is the failure to fully appreciate the distinction between affective and cognitive empathy. Second is an overestimation of the role of imagination in empathizing. Third is the failure to act on the difference between affective and cognitive empathizing. The authors use case studies to illustrate how to avoid these pitfalls in program design.

The fourth chapter, by Gerhard Minnameier, critically examines the theoretical background of empirical research on children's moral emotion expectancies within the happy victimizer paradigm. This paradigm has uncovered a developmental gap between these expectancies and moral cognition, with the former lagging behind the latter. The author questions whether the happy victimizer phenomenon is necessary to explain the gap between moral cognition and moral actions. In short, he critically examines whether the conceptual distinction that traditional theoretical approaches make between moral cognition and moral emotions is valid.

The volume concludes with a chapter by Darcia Narvaez, which presents an empirically derived model for moral education based on the Triune Ethics Theory (TET), a neurobiological theory of moral motivation that distinguishes three ethical orientations: security, engagement, and imagination. TET integrates virtue development, emphasizes the importance of emotion for moral functioning, and underscores the contribution of reasoning and deliberation for moral practice. Thus, TET provides an integrative framework for understanding the interplay between moral emotions and moral cognition across development.

In summary, by presenting new developmental and educational perspectives on the role of moral emotions and moral cognition in children's morality, this volume advances our understanding of children's moral development. In future research and educational practice, integrative approaches to children's morality promise to shed further light on our understanding of, and the promotion of, moral development in children.

References

Arsenio, W. (2008). Psychological limits of economic rationality: Relational contexts and cognitive irrationality. *Human Development*, *51*(4), 268–273.

Arsenio, W., Gold, J., & Adams, E. (2006). Children's conceptions and displays of moral emotions. In M. Killen & J. Smetana (Eds.), *Handbook of moral development* (pp. 581–610). Mahwah, NJ: Erlbaum.

Buxarrais, M. R., Martinez, M., Noguera, E., & Tey, A. (2003). Teachers evaluate the moral development of their students. In F. K. Oser & W. V. Veugelers (Eds.), *Teaching in moral and democratic education* (pp. 173–191). Bern, Switzerland: Peter Lang.

Edelstein, W. (2010). Werte und Kompetenzen für eine Schule der Demokratie. In B. Latzko & T. Malti (Eds.), *Moralische Entwicklung und Erziehung in Kindheit und Adoleszenz* [*Moral development and education in childhood and adolescence*]. (pp. 323–334). Göttingen, Germany: Hogrefe.

Eisenberg, N. (2000). Emotion, regulation, and moral development. *Annual Review of Psychology, 51*, 665–697.

Eisenberg, N., Spinrad, T. L., & Sadovsky, A. (2006). Empathy-related responding in children. In M. Killen & J. Smetana (Eds.), *Handbook of moral development* (pp. 517–549). Mahwah, NJ: Erlbaum.

Gasser, L., & Keller, M. (2009). Are the competent the morally good? Perspective taking and moral motivation of children involved in bullying. *Social Development*, *18*, 798–816.

Gummerum, M., Hanoch, Y., & Keller, M. (2008). When child development meets economic game theory: An interdisciplinary approach to investigating social development. *Human Development, 51*(4), 235–261.

Gutzwiller-Helfenfinger, E., Gasser, L., & Malti, T. (2010). Moral emotions and moral judgments in children's narratives: Comparing real-life and hypothetical transgressions. In B. Latzko & T. Malti (Eds.), *Children's moral emotions and moral cognition: Developmental and educational perspectives. New Directions for Child and Adolescent Development*, *129*, 11–31.

Harris, P. L. (1989). *Children and emotion*. New York: Cambridge University Press.

Helwig, C. C. (2008). The moral judgment of the child reevaluated. In C. Wainryb, J. G. Smetana, & E. Turiel (Eds.), *Social development, social inequalities, and social justice* (pp. 27–52). Mahwah, NJ: Erlbaum.

Hoffman, M. L. (2000). *Empathy and moral development: Implications for caring and justice*. Cambridge, MA: Cambridge University Press.

Keller, M. (1996). *Moralische Sensibilität: Entwicklung in Freundschaft und Familie* [*Moral sensitivity in friendship and family*]. Weinheim, Germany: Psychologie-Verlags Union.

Keller, M. (2004). Self in relationship. In D. K. Lapsley & D. Narvaez (Eds.), *Morality, self, and identity* (pp. 269–300). Mahwah, NJ: Erlbaum.

Killen, M., & Smetana, J. (Eds.). (2006). *Handbook of moral development*. Mahwah, NJ: Erlbaum.

Krettenauer, T., Malti, T., & Sokol, B. (2008). The development of moral emotion expectancies and the happy victimizer phenomenon: A critical review of theory and application. *European Journal of Developmental Science, 2*, 221–235.

Kochanska, G., Padavich, D. L., & Koenig, A. L. (1996). Children's narratives about hypothetical moral dilemmas and objective measures of their conscience: Mutual relations and socialization antecedents. *Child Development*, *67*, 1420–1436.

Kohlberg, L. (1984). *The psychology of moral development: The nature and validity of moral stages*. San Francisco: Harper and Row.

Latzko, B. (2008). No morality without autonomy: The role of emotional autonomy in moral development. In F. Oser & W. Veugelers (Eds.), *Getting involved: Global citizenship development and sources of moral values* (pp. 119–129). Rotterdam: Sense Publishers.

Latzko, B. (2010). Moral education in schools: Teachers´ authority and students´ autonomy. In C. Klaassen & N. Malovaty (Eds.), *Education for moral democracy in modern societies*. (pp. 91–102). Rotterdam: Sense Publishers.

Lind, G. (2010). Die Förderung moralisch-demokratischer Kompetenzen mit der Konstanzer Methode der Dilemma-Diskussion (KMDD) [The promotion of moral-democratic competencies using the Konstanz method of dilemma discussion]. In B. Latzko & T. Malti (Eds.), *Moralische Entwicklung und Erziehung in Kindheit und Adoleszenz [Moral development and education in childhood and adolescence]*. (pp. 285–301). Goettingen, Germany: Hogrefe.

Malti, T., Gasser, L., & Gutzwiller-Helfenfinger, E. (2010). Children's interpretive understanding, moral judgments, and emotion attributions: Relations to social behavior. *British Journal of Developmental Psychology.*

Malti, T., Gummerum, M., & Keller, M. (Eds.) (2008). Moral emotions and moral cognitions. *European Journal of Developmental Science, No. 2* (3).

Malti, T., Gummerum, M., Keller, M., & Buchmann, M. (2009). Children's moral motivation, sympathy, and prosocial behavior. *Child Development, 80,* 442–460.

Malti, T., & Keller, M. (in cooperation with F. X. Fang, A. Edele, & G. Sigurdardottir) (2010). Development of moral emotions in cultural context. In W. Arsenio & E. Lemerise (Eds.), *Emotions, aggression, and morality in children: Bridging development and psychopathology.* Washington, DC: American Psychological Association.

Maxwell, B., & DesRoches, S. (2010). Empathy and social-emotional learning: Pitfalls and touchstones for school-based programs. In B. Latzko & T. Malti (Eds.), *Children's moral emotions and moral cognition: Developmental and educational perspectives. New Directions for Child and Adolescent Development, 129*, 33–53.

Minnameier, G. (2010). The problem of moral motivation and the happy victimizer phenomenon: Killing two birds with one stone. In B. Latzko & T. Malti (Eds.), *Children's moral emotions and moral cognition: Developmental and educational perspectives. New Directions for Child and Adolescent Development, 129*, 55–75.

Narvaez, D. (2010). The emotional foundations of high moral intelligence. In B. Latzko & T. Malti (Eds.), Children's *moral emotions and moral cognition: Developmental and educational perspectives. New Directions for Child and Adolescent Development, 129*, 77–94.

Nucci, L.P., & Narvaez, D. (Eds.). (2008). *Handbook of moral and character education.* Mahwah, NJ: Erlbaum.

Nussbaum, M. (2001). *Upheavals of thought: The intelligence of emotions.* Cambridge, MA: Cambridge University Press.

Oser, F., Althof, W., & Higgins-D'Alessandro, A. (2008). The just community approach to moral education: System change or individual change? *Journal of Moral Education, 37*(3), 395–415.

Patry, J.-L., Weyringer, S., & Weinberger, A. (2007). Combining values and knowledge education. In D. N. Aspin & J. D. Chapman (Eds.), *Values education and lifelong learning* (pp. 160–179). Dordrecht: Springer.

Smetana, J. G., Campione-Barr, N., & Yell, N. (2003). Children's moral and affective judgments regarding provocation and retaliation. *Merrill-Palmer Quarterly, 49*(2), 209–236.

Smetana, J. G., & Killen, M. (2008). Moral cognition, emotion, and neuroscience: An integrative developmental view. *European Journal of Developmental Science*, 2, 324–339.

Tangney, J., Stuewig, J., & Mashek, D. (2007). Moral emotions, moral cognitions, and moral behavior. *Annual Review*, *58*, 345–372.

Turiel, E. (1983). *The development of social knowledge: Morality and Convention*. New York: Cambridge University Press.
Turiel, E. (in press). The development of morality: Reasoning, emotions, and resistance. In W. Overton (Ed.), *Handbook of lifespan human development*. New York: Wiley.

TINA MALTI is an assistant professor at the Department of Psychology at the University of Toronto Mississauga. E-mail: malti@jacobscenter.uzh.ch

BRIGITTE LATZKO is an assistant professor at the Faculty of Education, Department of Educational Psychology, at the University of Leipzig. E-mail: latzko@uni-leipzig.de

Gutzwiller-Helfenfinger, E., Gasser, L., & Malti, T. (2010). Moral emotions and moral judgments in children's narratives: Comparing real-life and hypothetical transgressions. In B. Latzko & T. Malti (Eds.), *Children's moral emotions and moral cognition: Developmental and educational perspectives. New Directions for Child and Adolescent Development, 129,* 11–31. San Francisco: Jossey-Bass.

2

Moral Emotions and Moral Judgments in Children's Narratives: Comparing Real-Life and Hypothetical Transgressions

Eveline Gutzwiller-Helfenfinger, Luciano Gasser, Tina Malti

Abstract

How children make meaning of their own social experiences in situations involving moral issues is central to their subsequent affective and cognitive moral learning. Our study of young children's narratives describing their interpersonal conflicts shows that the emotions and judgments constructed in the course of these real-life narratives differ from the emotions and judgments generated in the context of hypothetical transgressions. In the narratives, all emotions mentioned spontaneously were negative. In contrast, emotions attributed in the interview part covered a broader spectrum. One's own real-life transgressions were judged less severe and more justified than hypothetical transgressions. © Wiley Periodicals, Inc.

Emotions and cognitions experienced in real-life situations involving moral conflicts are an important source for children's moral learning (e.g., Malti & Latzko, this volume; Smetana & Killen, 2008). One promising methodological approach for gaining insight into how children reconstruct and attach meaning to their emotions and cognitions in social experiences is to use narratives of the child's own social experiences, especially when interpersonal conflicts and moral issues are involved (e.g., Wainryb, Brehl, & Matwin, 2005). According to Tappan (1991), narrative (storytelling) represents a central aspect of human existence and captures much of an individual's real-life moral experiences, including both personal (e.g., cognitive, emotional, conative) and contextual elements (e.g., gender, race, class, culture). In this chapter, we discuss children's moral emotions and judgments in a narrative context and compare them to emotions and judgments generated in the context of hypothetical transgressions. Such an analysis provides an improved understanding of how affective and cognitive aspects of sociomoral development are coordinated in different contexts.

Narratives and Moral Development

A narrative, defined as "the recounting of events" (Packer, 1991, p. 64), is constructed in such a way as to place these events in a particular narrative context, linking them coherently in time (Packer, 1991). Narratives are an essential tool for representing and interpreting human experience (Tappan, 1991), providing the experience with both shape and structure (Bruner, 1990). Narratives are embedded in the individual's culture and provide what Tappan (1991) calls "common discursive forestructures," which both guide individuals' interpretation and making sense of their actions and experiences over time, as well as "shape and organize those actions and experiences in the first place" (Tappan, 1991, p. 10; see also Gergen & Gergen, 1986). These forestructures can be conceptualized as mental representations of past experiences, which are activated in new situations and used as a framework for integrating (and interpreting) new experiences.

In this chapter, we focus on *personal narratives* as distinguished from scripts and stories (Hudson & Shapiro, 1991). Personal narratives are accounts of a person's own experiences and represent specific events. They are reported in the past tense and are told from the narrator's (i.e., first person) perspective (Hudson & Shapiro, 1991). Personal narratives derive their complexity from various sources, such as human cognitive organization, the narrator's characteristics, the influence of life experiences, and age (De Vries & Lehmann, 1996).

Narratives can be conceptualized as *reconstructions* of personal experiences. It is important to note that only what was salient at the time of the experience becomes part of a narrative (cf. Wainryb et al.,

2005). Narratives are thus not identical copies of all that happened, but structured representations of the salient features of those experiences (e.g., Tappan, 1991) or selective representations, including the individual's actual interpretation of the event at the time of telling (e.g., Bruner, 2002). We know that already small children make sense of and construct meaning from their experiences. By three years of age, children actively coconstruct their past experiences when conversing with adults, and by the end of preschool they can give fairly coherent accounts of their own (moral) experiences without adult guidance (McAdams, 2008). From early on, therefore, narratives indicate what features of an experience were salient to the child and were thus integrated into the child's interpretation of the situation, thereby providing the foundation for future behavior.

What functions do narratives serve in moral development? First, they can "provide powerful models of moral behavior" (Tappan, 1998, p. 151), as well as express and represent a person's moral experience consisting of real-life moral conflicts and dilemmas (Tappan, 1998). For example, one might tell a child the story about the boy who cried "wolf" to illustrate how important it is to tell the truth. In this tale, the fact that no wolf came when the boy first claimed its presence led the adults in the village not to believe him when the wolf really did appear and ate all the sheep. Telling children how guilty someone felt after stealing candy from a shop helps them see that stealing is not okay and makes one feel bad. Taking a Vygotskian and sociocultural perspective, Tappan (2006) proposes a "meditational" position that stresses the *mediatory and shaping* function of narratives: Narratives not only provide a structural framework for integrating and assigning meaning to moral experiences (see also Narvaez, this volume), but also mediate and shape these experiences in critical ways. In this sense, narratives operate as a cultural tool through which these experiences can be expressed, thereby adapting them to the child's particular narrative culture and tradition by using the symbols and discursive forms that the culture provides.

Day's (1991) concept of the *moral audience* is related to this mediatory function. According to this view, individuals, while telling narratives about their own moral experiences, also construct an internalized audience that includes both real and imaginary persons who represent specific moral principles; these persons then "judge" the experiences. Accordingly, both the internalized moral audience and the real audience (i.e., the actual listener) are important social counterparts or "coplayers" because they give meaning to the moral experience. However, moral development shaped through narratives involves not only a moral audience, but also a *moral self*, which according to Day and Tappan's (1996) approach is referred to as a "dialogical self." This dialogical self is constructed socially and intersubjectively and is by its very nature relational. Moral life is aimed at understanding and managing the relationships among the ongoing dialogues that occur between (and within) actors, as well as among their stories. This relational aspect stresses the central role narratives play in interviewees' self-reports of the real-life moral conflicts and dilemmas they have faced (cf. Day & Tappan, 1996).

Accordingly, *moral internalization* can be seen as part of this ongoing dialogue, the result of an individual's active transformation and reconstruction of language and discourse into new forms of inner speech, that is, the individual's own inner moral thought and language (cf. Tappan, 1998). Moral norms, rules, and values are thus part of this socially and culturally based language and discourse, and their different meanings are both coconstructed and reconstructed during internal and external dialogical interactions.

Narratives and Understanding Moral Emotions

Moral emotions are considered to be a key element of human moral experience. They also may be key to understanding why individuals adhere or fail to adhere to their own moral standards (Tangney, Stuewig, & Mashek, 2007). Haidt (2003) described moral emotions as those "that are linked to the interests or welfare either of society as a whole or at least of persons other than the judge or agent" (p. 853). Tangney et al. (2007) distinguished between self-conscious moral emotions (shame, guilt, embarrassment, and moral pride) and other-focused moral emotions (righteous anger, contempt, disgust, elevation, and gratitude). Moreover, they discussed other-oriented empathy as a morally relevant emotional process with both affective and cognitive components (Eisenberg, 2000; Hoffman, 2000; for an in-depth discussion of empathy see Maxwell & DesRoches, this volume). We, as well as other researchers, have argued that moral emotions are inevitably associated with moral cognitions because emotions such as sympathy are based on an understanding of the other person's circumstances and constitute the basic motive in situations calling for moral actions (e.g., Eisenberg, 2000; Malti, Gasser, & Gutzwiller-Helfenfinger, 2010).

What role does emotion, especially moral emotion, play in narratives? Although moral emotions are not specifically addressed in the literature on narrative development, Nicolopoulou (1997) has emphasized the central role emotions play in narrative development. The impact of a narrative is primarily due to both the "extent to which it can engage both speakers and listeners *emotionally*" (Nicolopoulou, 1997, p. 201) and the ways individuals can use it symbolically to express and handle situations and themes that move (i.e., fascinate, perplex, or trouble) them emotionally. Effective narratives embody the interplay between cognitive processes and emotional life, such that they "can be used to mobilize emotions for cognitive ends" (Nicolopoulou, 1997, p. 201).We can therefore assume that the more a narrative engages the speaker and listener emotionally, the more attention it receives, and the higher the probability that the plot will be integrated into the listener's narrative repertoire. The theme of the narrative can then be used to convey the specific interpretation and emotional valence attached to it. When similar situations or experiences (or narratives about them) are encountered, that narrative and its meaning can be retrieved, thereby providing an interpretative framework for integrating the new situation. In other words, the narrative is used as a discursive fore-structure. This ongoing process of creating structures of meaning and using and further adaptation of the structures can be conceptualized as the assimilation and accommodation of schemata, as described by Piaget (e.g., Piaget, 1967).

What about the *emotional engagement* mentioned by Nicolopoulou (1997)? Emotions give meaning and valence to interactions, actions, and events (Ellsworth & Scherer, 2003), either accompanying the actor's actions (e.g., feeling happy while playing the piano) or following it, and they apply both to the actor and the person to whom the action is directed (e.g., a child feels happy after grabbing another child's candy, and the other child feels sad about losing the candy). Even the anticipation of an action (either by the actor or the recipient) can be accompanied by emotions (e.g., a girl feeling happy because she knows she is going to watch a TV show, or feeling afraid because she knows she will be scolded for losing her sister's doll). Accordingly, actual and inferred emotions can give meaning to actions and events by serving as signposts that direct an individual's attention to the things that seem important (cf. Nicolopoulou, 1997).

Moreover, because actions and events—as they are normally told to others—are often organized as narratives, the emotions these narratives *include* also have meaning and significance for both the speaker and the listener. Accordingly, both the inclusion and omission of emotions in a narrative, as well as the nature of the emotions when they are included, provide important additional information about the judgments and evaluations children make in these contexts. They also influence how the narrative is interpreted. In a transgression context, whether or not emotions are included, and if they are, whether both the perpetrator and victim are endowed with emotions can guide the listener's interpretation of the transgression, as well as its severity and consequences. Stating a mere fact, such as "He had a toy I wanted so I took it," provides minimal information and says nothing about what aspects of the situation are being emphasized. The following two descriptions of that same situation can emphasize different aspects. Consider the statements, "He had a toy I wanted, and I was so angry he would not give it to me that I just took it" and "He had a toy I wanted, so I took it, and he was so sad he started crying." The first statement gives the perpetrator's perspective and explains the urge to grab the toy, perhaps hinting at the extenuating circumstance of the victim refusing to hand over the toy. The second statement conveys the emotional state of the victim caused by the perpetrator's action, thereby acknowledging the victim's suffering. Thus, the emotions a narrator ascribes to the protagonist direct the listener's attention to those aspects of the situation that the narrator wants to emphasize, thereby dictating the listener's interpretation of the situation. When no emotions are mentioned, as in the first statement, the account is more matter-of-fact, indicating that the narrator is not emphasizing or even paying attention to emotions. This is often the case in the narratives of young children, because the understanding of one's own emotions and the emotions of others, as well as the relation between emotions and the accompanying mental states or thought processes, develops in the preschool and early primary school years (e.g., Flavell, Flavell, & Green, 2001).

From a *moral development perspective*, moral emotions are important in several respects. First, moral emotions indicate that moral events are more salient than nonmoral events and are thus central to the development of moral judgments (Smetana & Killen, 2008) and moral motivation (Nunner-Winkler, 2007). Second, a child's immediate moral emotional reaction to a moral rule violation indicates the importance the child assigns to the moral issues involved (Malti, Gummerum, Keller, & Buchmann, 2009). Accordingly, when children include moral emotions (e.g., guilt) in their narrative accounts of their interpersonal conflicts, we can interpret this inclusion as representing their moral sensitivity to the moral aspects of the situation (cf. Gasser & Keller, 2009; Malti et al., in press). Thus, bearing in mind (a) the power of narratives to engage both speakers and listeners emotionally; (b) the "tool character" of narratives as a way of constructing, integrating, and conveying meaning; and (c) Nicolopoulou's (1997) tenet that effective narratives are an embodiment of the interplay between cognitive processes and emotional life, studying children's narratives helps elucidate just this interplay, which is central to moral functioning.

The above is in line with recent trends in the sociocognitive research literature, particularly the call for a more integrative developmental view of moral judgments and moral emotions (Arsenio & Lemerise, 2004; Arsenio, Gold, & Adams, 2006; Smetana & Killen, 2008). Accordingly, children judge moral transgressions negatively because they experience them as emotionally salient, and they associate moral emotions such as sympathy with these transgressions (Arsenio & Lemerise, 2004). Thus, children's moral judgments are essential to morality, whereas moral emotions, particularly sympathy, are assumed to help children anticipate the negative outcomes of moral transgressions and coordinate their moral action tendencies accordingly (Malti, Gasser, & Buchmann, 2009).

Development of Children's Understanding of Moral Emotions

Central to the developmental approach to moral emotions is the study of emotions that children expect will result from various (im)moral acts, as well as how these emotion expectancies influence their moral judgments and eventual behavior (Arsenio et al. 2006; Krettenauer, Malti, & Sokol, 2008). Within this approach, the decrease in the attribution of future positive emotions to perpetrators (i.e., a decrease in the happy victimizer phenomenon) signals an important developmental transition in children's emotion understanding (Arsenio et al., 2006). This transition, which takes place around age six or seven years, involves a child understanding that immoral conduct causes a transgressor to feel sad, guilty, or remorseful. The core question is why young children, despite having already developed an intrinsic understanding of moral rules by age three or four years, still lack the corresponding emotional morality (Lourenço, 1997). In other words, young children attribute positive rather than negative feelings to victimizers (Krettenauer et al., 2008). Several studies have elucidated the role of moral emotion expectancies or attributions in causing (mal)adaptive behavior. These studies underscore the value of considering emotional processes in explaining moral functioning (e.g., Gasser & Keller, 2009; Krettenauer & Eichler, 2006; Malti et al., 2009; Malti et al., 2010).

To further explore the role of emotions and judgments in children's moral development, and especially the happy victimizer phenomenon, we propose a complementary, narrative approach. The emotions that are generated in children when they produce a narrative about their own moral transgression can be conceptualized as *reconstructed emotions*. As such, they are assumed to represent the aspects of the situation that are salient to the child. Such reconstructed emotions can then be contrasted with the emotion expectancies generated during a subsequent interview. Previous research by Wainryb et al. (2005) examined only the emotions that are actively produced during a narrative; it did not systematically assess the emotion expectancies attributed to both perpetrator and victim in the narrative. The assessment of both the reconstructed emotions and emotion expectancies referring to the same real-life situation can provide separate insights into children's understanding of the emotional aspects of their own moral transgressions.

We also wanted to examine potential differences between the emotions attributed to both perpetrators and victims in narratives of real-life events compared to those attributed in the context of hypothetical scenarios. To date, it seems that no such comparison has been undertaken, although a study by Smetana et al. (1999) is a step in the right direction. Comparing hypothetical transgressions to actual classroom transgressions, Smetana et al. (1999) assessed maltreated and nonmaltreated preschool children's emotion expectancies for both the transgressor and the victim. The children were (a) presented with six hypothetical transgressions, and (b) interviewed about naturally occurring events in their classrooms and had to say how both the transgressor and the victim felt when the transgression occurred. Even though no differences were found in the children's affective responses to the hypothetical and real-life situations, their moral judgments and justifications differed in the two contexts. Specifically, the hypothetical situations were viewed as deserving more punishment than the real-life situations. Moreover, the children focused more on the intrinsic consequences of the transgressions for others when justifying the perpetrator's conduct in hypothetical situations, but they were less able to justify why the transgression was wrong in the real-life scenario than in the hypothetical scenario. To Smetana et al. (1999), these findings confirm the earlier proposition (e.g., Smetana et al., 1993) that events contextualized in real-life social interactions require children to consider, weigh, and coordinate factors such as their relationship with the victim or the perpetrator, potential extenuating circumstances, and the potential consequences of their actions; these considerations then influence the children's judgments.

Because narratives can be conceptualized as *representations of contextualized social interactions*, we can assume that moral judgments and emotion expectancies, as well as their justifications, are different for narratives of real-life situations than for hypothetical scenarios. Moreover, real-life situations are more complex than hypothetical situations because, in addition to the moral considerations, perpetrators must justify their own transgressions by referring to their own goals (Wainryb et al., 2005). These authors demonstrated that when narratives were told from the perpetrator's perspective as compared to the victim's perspective, the children were required to pay more attention to the transgressor's goals, and they were more engaged in coordinating their intentions with the inferred perspective of the victim. Because these children coordinated different and partly contradictory aspects of their own behavior (talking about harming someone while simultaneously trying to maintain a positive moral self-image), their narratives were less coherent; that is, they included various shifts between the perpetrator's (the narrator's) and the victim's perspectives (Wainryb et al., 2005). Thus, providing a narrative about one's own transgression is a highly demanding task, which requires the inclusion of rich, contextualized information with the self as the central agent. This complexity prevents the narrator from engaging in the more objective reflection processes involved in hypothetical situations. In hypothetical situations, on the other hand, the child is primarily concerned about the harmful consequences of the moral transgression and can concentrate on this central issue without having to establish and maintain a primarily positive self-image.

Studying Children's Narratives

Two broad approaches to the study of children's sociomoral narratives can be distinguished. The first approach uses narratives of real-life experiences based on actual behavior, as well as the reconstructed emotions and thoughts that the behavior engenders. This is the approach presented so far in this chapter (e.g., Day & Tappan, 1996; Hudson & Shapiro, 1991; Tappan, 1991; 1998; Wainryb et al., 2005). The second approach uses *hypothetical narratives*, that is, narratives elicited after presenting children with standardized story beginnings, to assess their declarative knowledge. This approach, commonly used in attachment research, provides insight into children's emotions, thoughts, and action tendencies. To elicit these narratives, standardized story stems (i.e., beginnings) have been used (MacArthur Story Stem Battery [MSSB]; e.g., Bretherton, Prentiss, & Ridgeway, 1990). In conducting moral development research, Kochanska, Padavich, and Koenig (1996) adapted these story stems to include moral stems (cf. Ramos-Marcuse & Arsenio, 2001; Waldinger, Toth, & Gerber, 2001). This latter approach is not described in more depth here because it does not use the assessment of personal experiences to tap children's understanding of social situations, but uses instead stories produced on the basis of standardized cues. For a comprehensive overview of this approach, see Emde, Wolf, and Oppenheim (2003).

The features and functions of personal narratives presented so far show that narratives are an ideal way to capture the multidimensional aspects of moral experience. Time, place, actors, actions (behavior), relationships, intentions, motives, and emotions are not only the basic elements of a moral experience, but also the elements of a narrative. Narratives—as cognitive and sociocultural forestructures—enable individuals to meaningfully organize these elements to interpret their moral experiences, to reflect on them, and to use them as a basis for subsequent behavior. Accordingly, the research method of eliciting personal moral narratives can provide insight into these individual construals by showing what features of children's social interactions are salient to them and subsequently form the basis for understanding them. As recognition of the salient features of situations and experiences is the basis for subsequent moral judgments and the development of moral understanding (Wainryb et al., 2005), gaining access to these narrative construals helps the researcher identify the "raw materials of which moral development is made up" (Wainryb et al., 2005, p.2). Moreover, in accordance with Day's (1991) concept of the moral audience, children giving narratives to adult researchers may strive to present themselves as morally "good" and thus construct the narrative to correspond with the moral principles they assume the adults adhere to. We may also speculate that already in preschool, children attempt to construct moral self-consistency, which can form the basis for later development of a moral self. As a consequence, and in line with Smetana et al.'s (1999) conception of contextualization, we may expect that children consider the real-life transgressions that they report in narratives to be less severe than hypothetical transgressions, and that the justifications for their moral judgments differ accordingly. Thus, we may speculate that real-life transgressions might be justified as more excusable and thus less subject to moral standards.

Wainryb et al.'s (2005) seminal study of children's narratives and the moral judgments they make about their interpersonal conflicts shows that narratives are indeed well suited to unveiling those aspects of social situations that form the basis of children's moral understanding and development. Their core findings demonstrate that when children and adolescents produce narrative accounts and moral evaluations of their own interpersonal conflicts involving moral transgressions, one from the perspective of the victim and one from the perspective of the perpetrator, the content and coherence of the accounts vary as a function of this perspective, as do the moral evaluations. The victim narratives were mainly self-referential: They referred to the narrator's experience and were more coherent than the perpetrator narratives, which frequently shifted between references to the narrator's own experience and the other's experience. Moreover, in the victim narratives, the children mostly judged the transgressions to be wrong. In contrast, in the perpetrator narratives, almost half of the moral judgments were positive or mixed (right or both right and wrong). However, the perpetrator narratives were just as long and detailed as the victim narratives, and they referred to similar types of harmful behavior (Wainryb et al., 2005). These systematic effects of perspective on both narrative interpretations and moral judgments highlight the importance of including children's interpretations of their social interactions in the study of moral understanding and development, as these interpretations are the basis of moral thinking (cf. Wainryb et al., 2005).

Wainryb et al. (2005) reported that the narrator's emotions were present in 35 percent of the perpetrator narratives, but the other person's were present in 71 percent. In contrast, the narrator's emotions were present in 67 percent of the victim narratives and the other child's emotions in only 16 percent. Generally, the victim narratives centered mainly on emotions, whereas intentions were predominant in the perpetrator narratives. Thus, to perpetrators, the other child's (i.e., the victim's) emotions were more salient and relevant than their own, thereby emphasizing the victim's emotional reaction to the transgression. Accordingly, the emotions attributed to the perpetrator were mainly guilt and anger. Guilt appeared significantly more often in the perpetrator narratives than in the victim narratives, whereas the victims more often described themselves as feeling sad or generally unwell (unelaborated negative emotions). Inclusion of both the narrator's and the other person's emotions increased with age (Wainryb et al., 2005). However, as the sample was cross-sectional, the elucidation of developmental trends awaits longitudinal studies.

The currently available findings thus show that children spontaneously refer to both their own and the other's emotional state, and that the emotions reflected in narratives—sadness, guilt, and anger—are moral or morally relevant. In cases where no specific moral emotion was mentioned, references were made to unelaborated *negative* feelings, mainly in the victim. Thus, the evidence shows that children are aware that real-life moral transgressions cause both specific and nonspecific negative feelings in both the victim and the perpetrator.

Our Empirical Study: Children's Narratives of Their Own Moral Transgressions

We now present our own research on preschool and primary school children's narratives of their own interpersonal conflicts involving a moral transgression, addressing the role of both moral emotions and moral judgments. Our primary research questions were the following: (a) Which moral emotions attributed to self (perpetrator) and other (victim) are mentioned, both spontaneously and after prompting, in preschool and schoolchildren's narratives of harming another child? In accordance with Wainryb et al.'s (2005) findings, we expected the children to mention mainly negative emotions, especially guilt, anger, and sadness. (b) What motives for transgression do the children mention spontaneously in their narratives? (c) What justifications do the children give in their narratives for both their emotion attributions and moral judgments? (d) How do moral judgments and emotion attributions, and their justifications, differ as a function of whether the events are real or hypothetical? Based on Smetana et al.'s (1999) findings, we expected that both judgments and justifications would be based to a greater extent on moral principles if the transgressions are hypothetical.

We made no predictions regarding emotion expectancies and their justifications. We assumed that by prompting standardized emotions in the interview following the narrative, the constructed, real-life character of the narrative would be partly lost. The task of evaluating each emotion acquires a more hypothetical character, because if a particular emotion is not mentioned spontaneously in the narrative, we must assume that it is not part of the child's reconstruction of the situation. Thus, this task is very similar to evaluating the emotions attributed to the characters in a hypothetical scenario. Accordingly, it was not clear whether children's emotion attributions would differ in the real-life narratives and in the hypothetical scenarios.

Method

General Procedure. We developed a method to elicit children's narratives of their own moral transgressions based on that used by Wainryb et al. (2005). After eliciting the narrative, we used a half-standardized interview to probe (a) the children's motives, (b) their moral judgments, (c) their justifications for these judgments, (d) the emotions they attribute to both themselves and others, and (e) their justifications for the emotions attributed to the self. The children were also presented with two hypothetical scenarios of moral transgressions. They had to (a) morally judge these transgressions, (b) justify their judgments, (c) attribute emotions to both the perpetrator and the victim, and (d) justify the emotions attributed to the perpetrator.

Participants. The sample consisted of 190 Swiss preschool and school children. There were 92 girls and 98 boys, 59 of whom (25 girls and 34 boys) were ca. five years old ($M = 5.5$) and 131 of whom (67 girls and 64 boys) were ca. nine years old ($M = 9.5$ years). The children attended kindergarten and primary school, respectively. Their socioeconomic status was representative of the German-speaking part of Switzerland.

Real-Life Narratives. One narrative was elicited from each participant. The children were asked to talk about a situation where they—as perpetrator—did or said something that hurt another child: "Now you may tell me something that happened to you, and I am going to listen first and ask you some questions afterwards. Tell me about a time when you did or said something, and a child you know well ended up feeling hurt by it. Pick a time that you remember really well, and tell me everything that you remember about that time."

The researchers allowed the participants to give their narratives without interruption, making no comments and asking no questions. Thus, the participants talked until they reached the end of their respective narratives, indicated by keeping silent or making a brief comment such as "that's it." At that point, the researcher asked, "Is there anything else you remember about that time?" This procedure ensured that the researcher did not provide any cues that could influence the content or structure of the narrative (cf. Wainryb et al., 2005). If the children did not mention a motive for their harmful actions, the researchers asked them why they had acted this way. If the harmful action was not described clearly (e.g., "I just did something..."), the researcher asked what exactly the child had done. These two probes were included to ensure that both the motive for and the nature of the harmful action were made explicit.

After the narrative, the interview began. The researchers asked the children to morally judge the harmful act they described in their narratives and to justify these judgments. If the children judged the acts to be wrong, they were asked to rate how serious the transgression was. Afterwards, the children were asked to tell the researcher both how they felt after harming the other child and how the other child felt. The child also had to justify the moral emotion attributed to the self.

Hypothetical Scenarios. The same interview procedure was used for the two hypothetical transgression scenarios as for the real-life narratives, but data collection took place on a different day. The participants were told two stories, each containing a moral transgression representing typical overtly aggressive behavior: physical (hitting) and verbal attacks (teasing). The stories were illustrated with colored pictures and matched for the child's sex. Again, the children were prompted for moral judgments and their justification, degree of seriousness, emotions attributed to the perpetrator and victim, and justification of the emotion attributed to the perpetrator.

Coding of Real-Life Narratives. The number of occurrences of each narrative element was noted. The coding procedure was based on Wainryb et al. (2005).

Narrative Elements. The following *moral emotions* were coded for both self (perpetrator) and other (victim): sadness, guilt, anger, unspecified negative, and other emotions (e.g., jealousy, anxiety, hurt feelings). The perpetrator's *justifications* for harmful acts were coded as follows: (a) deontic (refers to moral norms and rules), (b) empathic (mentions the victim's plight), (c) sanction-oriented (mentions praise, blame, or punishment by others), (d) hedonistic (mentions satisfying a personal need), (e) legitimate (mentions a harmful reaction to provocation), (f) alternative action (mentions nonaggressive alternatives), (g) repetition of the harmful act (repeats mention of the act), (h) guilt (mentions feelings of guilt or a bad conscience), and (i) undifferentiated or inappropriate justifications (e.g., "I just did it").

The perpetrator's *motives* were coded as follows: (a) instrumental goal (acts harmfully to pursue own goals); (b) vengeance (feels provoked); (c) false assumption (recognizes own misconstrual of the situation, which nonetheless was the basis for the harmful behavior); (d) impulsivity (acts out of anger, jealousy, or frustration); (e) harmful intent (wants to harm the victim and does not care about the victim's welfare); (f) accidental (intends no harm); (g) fun (mentions fun as the motive); and (h) incomprehensible (gives no reasons for the harmful behavior).

Both the justification and the motive codings were dichotomized: If a category was used, the element was coded as 1, if not, it was coded as 0. To account for narrative length, the number of words in the narrative, including the answers to probes within the narrative phase, was counted for each narrative.

Coding of Moral Judgments, Emotion Attributions, Justifications for Both Real-Life and Hypothetical Transgressions. Moral judgments, emotion attributions, and justifications of judgments and attributions were coded identically for both the real-life and hypothetical transgressions. *Moral judgment* was coded as 0 if the child said that it was okay and 1 if the child said it was wrong to transgress. In the latter case, the child had to indicate how *serious* the transgression was: The judgment was coded as 1 if the transgression was described as only a little bad and 2 if it was described as being very bad.

The coding of justifications for moral judgments was identical to the coding of spontaneous justifications for harmful acts. The emotion categories (happy, angry, sad, fearful, neutral) were dichotomized, with 1 indicating that the emotion had been attributed and 0 indicating that it had not been attributed.

Twenty of the narratives (16 percent) were fully coded by two raters. Interrater reliability was good, with 84 percent agreement on the narrative elements (Cohen's $\kappa = .74$).

Results

Real-Life Narratives. Of the 190 children tested, 126 (60 girls and 66 boys) produced codable narratives. Of the remaining 64, 20 had nothing to tell, 38 told stories that did not involve them harming another child, and 6 gave narratives that were flawed due to incorrect assessments. Of the 126 children whose narratives were valid and included for analysis, 27 (21.4 percent) were five years old and 99 (78.6 percent) were nine years old.

Eighty-six (68.3 percent) of the narratives were told from a retaliatory point of view in that the perpetrators stated that they had been provoked. In the remaining 40 narratives (31.7 percent), no initial provocation was mentioned, and they were labeled as prototypic. The number of words in the narratives ranged from 7 to 169 ($M = 47.6$, $SD = 34$). The nine-year-olds told significantly longer narratives than the five-year-olds ($M = 53.93$ vs. $M = 24.33$).

Moral Emotions. Moral emotions were mentioned in 50 of the 126 narratives (39.7 percent). In 35 narratives (27.8 percent), only one emotion was mentioned; in 8 (6.3 percent), two; in 4 (3.2 percent), three; and in 3 (2.4 percent), four were mentioned.

In all but one of the prototypic narratives, all the spontaneously mentioned emotions were negative, regardless of whether they were attributed to the self (perpetrator) or the other (victim). In the one prototypic narrative where a positive emotion was mentioned, the victim was described as feeling content after the perpetrator had apologized and made amends.

Regarding the perpetrator's emotions, sadness was mentioned in three narratives (2.4 percent); guilt was mentioned in seven narratives (5.6 percent); anger was mentioned in fourteen narratives (11.1 percent); undifferentiated, negative emotions were mentioned once (0.8 percent); and other negative emotions were also mentioned once (0.8 percent). For the victim, sadness was mentioned in twenty-two narratives (17.5 percent), anger in eight (6.4 percent), and other negative emotions in six (4.8 percent). Guilt and undifferentiated negative emotions were never mentioned. Moral emotions were mentioned significantly more often by nine-year-olds than by five-year-olds ($M = .71$ vs. $M = .19$).

Motives for Spontaneously Mentioned Transgressions. All but one of the motive categories (harmful intent) were mentioned. The most frequently mentioned motive was vengeance (sixty-six instances), followed by impulsivity (eleven), and instrumental goals (eight). Accidental, fun, and incomprehensible motives were mentioned five times each, and a false assumption was stated twice. Overall, some kind of motive was mentioned in ninety-three narratives (74.8 percent). In seventy-nine narratives (62.7 percent), only one motive was mentioned; in thirteen (10.3 percent), two were mentioned; and in 1 (1.0 percent), four were mentioned.

Emotions Attributed to Perpetrator and Victim After Prompting. When the children were asked directly to attribute moral emotions both to the perpetrator (self) and to the victim (other) during the interview part of the session, they distributed their attributions as follows. Regarding the perpetrator (self), fourteen participants (11.1 percent) attributed happiness; twenty-two (17.5 percent), anger; forty-nine (38.9 percent), sadness; twelve (9.5 percent), fear; and seventeen (13.5 percent), neutral emotions. Twelve (9.5 percent) participants either gave no answer or mentioned undifferentiated negative emotions. To the victim (other), fifteen children (11.9 percent) attributed happiness; twenty-seven (21.4 percent), anger; fifty-four (42.9 percent), sadness; eleven (8.7 percent), fear; and nine (7.1 percent), neutral emotions. Ten participants either gave no answer or attributed undifferentiated negative emotions.

Justifications of Moral Judgments and Emotions Attributed to the Perpetrator (Self). With respect to moral judgments, 19 children (15.1 percent) said it was okay to harm the other child, but 104 (82.5 percent) said it was wrong. Three children made no judgments at all. The predominant justification categories were deontic, empathic, sanction-oriented, and legitimate. Deontic justifications were more frequent for judgments (21 percent) than for emotion attributions (10 percent). A quarter of the children (25 percent) mentioned empathic justifications in the judgment context and 10 percent in the emotion attribution context. Only 4 percent referred to sanctions in the judgment context, whereas 21 percent mentioned them in the emotion attribution context. In the judgment context, 18 percent mentioned legitimate justifications, whereas in the emotion attribution context 12 percent referred to it.

Comparing Real-Life Narratives and Hypothetical Scenarios. In keeping with previous research, we computed several measures of judgments, attributions, and justifications for both real-life narratives and hypothetical scenarios. Children's combined moral and severity judgments were coded as 1 (okay), 2 (serious), and 3 (very serious). For two justification categories, former categories were collapsed: (a) moral: others' welfare or the unfairness of the action (merging of deontic, empathic, and guilt), and (b) undifferentiated (merging of repetition of harmful act and undifferentiated/inappropriate). Sanction-oriented, legitimate, hedonistic, and alternative action were left unchanged (cf. Smetana et al., 2003). To account for multiple justifications, the mean proportion of each type of justification was calculated for each child.

To analyze severity judgments, emotion attributions, and their justifications, separate mixed ANOVAs were performed, with gender and age (five- vs. nine-year-olds) as the between-groups factors and context

Table 2.1. Mean Proportional Scores and Standard Deviations for the Dependent Variables in Real-Life (Narratives) versus Hypothetical Scenarios as a Function of Age

	Real-Life		*Hypothetical*	
	5 Years	*9 Years*	*5 Years*	*9 Years*
Moral judgment (severity)	1.00 (0.00)	2.14 (.70)	2.25 (.35)	2.54 (.40)
Justifications of moral judgment (merged categories)				
Moral	.16 (.17)	.17 (.17)	.70 (.44)	.95 (.15)
Legitimate	.07 (.27)	.20 (.40)	.00 (.00)	.01 (.05)
Alternative action	.07 (.27)	.07 (.26)	.00 (.00)	.01 (.08)
Emotions attributed to perpetrator				
Fear[a]	.04 (.21)	.12 (.33)	.09 (.19)	.25 (.34)
Justifications of emotion attributions to perpetrator (merged categories)				
Moral	.07 (.14)	.09 (.15)	.15 (.36)	.38 (.39)
Sanction-oriented	.11 (.32)	.24 (.43)	.30 (.44)	.45 (.39)
Legitimate	.00 (.00)	.15 (.36)	.02 (.10)	.01 (.07)
Hedonistic	.00 (.00)	.00 (.00)	.04 (.19)	.03 (.14)
Undifferentiated	.09 (.20)	.10 (.24)	.28 (.45)	.11 (.24)

[a]A significant effect involving context was found for fear only.

(narrative vs. hypothetical scenarios) as the within-groups factor. Only the significant main effects for context and interaction effects including context are reported. The means are displayed in Table 2.1.

Severity Judgments. A significant main effect for context was found. Children judged hypothetical transgressions more severely than their own transgressions.

Justifications for Moral Judgments. A significant main effect for context was found. Children gave more justifications for moral judgments of hypothetical than real-life transgressions. This main effect was superseded by a significant Age × Context interaction, with older children giving more moral justifications than younger children for hypothetical transgressions.

A significant context effect was also found for *legitimate* justifications. Children more often referred to legitimate justifications for real-life than for hypothetical transgressions. The same context effect was found for *alternative action*. Children more often referred to an alternative strategy when the transgression was real-life than when it was hypothetical.

Finally, a significant context effect was found for *undifferentiated* justifications. Children gave more such justifications for hypothetical than for real-life transgressions. This main effect was superseded by a significant Age × Context interaction, indicating that the younger children gave more undifferentiated justifications than the older children for hypothetical transgressions.

Emotions Attributed to Perpetrator. Only for *fear* was a significant Gender × Age × Context interaction found. In the hypothetical context, nine-year-old girls attributed more fear to the perpetrator than nine-year-old boys.

Justification of Emotions Attributed to Perpetrator. For *moral justifications*, a significant main effect for context was found. Children gave more moral justifications for the emotions they attributed to the perpetrator if the transgression was hypothetical than if it was real-life. This main effect was superseded by a significant Age × Context interaction, showing that older children gave more moral justifications than younger children for hypothetical transgressions.

A significant main effect for context was found for *sanction-oriented* justifications. Children gave more sanction-oriented justifications for hypothetical transgressions than for real-life transgressions. For *legitimate* justifications, a significant Age × Context interaction was found, indicating that nine-year-olds used legitimate justifications more often than five-year-olds if the transgression was hypothetical.

For *hedonistic* justifications, a main effect for context was found. Children gave more hedonistic justifications for hypothetical transgressions than for real-life transgressions. For *undifferentiated* justifications, a main effect for context was also found. Children gave more undifferentiated justifications for hypothetical than for real-life transgressions. This main effect was superseded by a significant Age × Context interaction, indicating that younger children gave more undifferentiated justifications than older children for hypothetical transgressions.

Narrative, Moral Emotions, and Moral Cognition: Concluding Remarks

The aim of this chapter was first to integrate our research findings with the literature on both narrative and moral development, and second, to emphasize the importance of merging moral emotions and moral cognitions (cf. Malti & Latzko, this volume). We argue that the way children construct and—by narrating them—reconstruct the meaning of their own interpersonal encounters in morally relevant situations represents a central vantage point for their development of a concern for others. This concern may then become part of their moral self.

Our results indicate that for a majority of the children (68 percent), the real-life narratives were retaliatory; that is, the children reported acting as perpetrators in situations where they felt provoked by the other party, an interpretation they used to legitimize their own harmful acts. The remaining 32 percent were set in a so-called prototypic context that involved no visible provocation on the part of the victim. Except for one prototypic narrative, all the *spontaneously* mentioned emotions were negative, regardless of whether they were attributed to the self (perpetrator) or the other (victim). Also, the nine-year-old school children reported more of these emotions than the five-year-old preschool children. Whereas anger and guilt were the emotions most frequently attributed to the perpetrator, sadness was the predominant emotion attributed to the victim. These results correspond well to Wainryb et al.'s (2005) findings, and they show that, in the context of moral transgressions, the emotions produced spontaneously in children's narratives are *always* morally relevant; that is, they are moral emotions. Moreover, no indications of the happy victimizer phenomenon were found, as all emotions attributed to the perpetrator were negative.

In the interview per se, the variety of response choices offered allowed a broad spectrum of moral emotions to be attributed to both perpetrator and victim. For perpetrators as well as victims, the predominant emotion attributed was sadness. Satisfaction, fear, and neutral emotions were also attributed to both perpetrator and victim, even though these emotions were never mentioned in the narratives. These findings reveal that different pictures emerged about the details the children provided when talking about the same (personal) moral transgressions, depending on the method used to elicit the information. Thus, the narratives yielded a relatively narrow spectrum of exclusively negative emotions, whereas the interviews yielded a broader spectrum that included both positive and neutral emotions as well as negative emotions.

When the moral judgments, emotion attributions, and justifications given in the context of real-life and hypothetical transgressions were compared, distinct patterns emerged. Both main effects and interactions were found involving context (real-life or hypothetical), and the interactions mostly involved age. Hypothetical transgressions were judged by all the children to be more severe and were given more moral justifications (by the older children) and more undifferentiated justifications (by the younger children) than were real-life transgressions. Conversely, real-life transgressions were more often presented as justified or legitimate, whereas moral judgments were more often justified by proposing an alternative strategy, indicating that when children refer to their own transgressions, they try to present themselves as morally intact by eliminating or attenuating inconsistencies between their actions and their claims to be moral persons. This result is in line with Day's (1991) conception of narratives as giving the narrator a moral audience, as well as research investigating the role of narratives in developing moral self and a moral identity (e.g., Day & Tappan, 1996; McAdams, 2008): Both require narrators to present themselves as basically "good" and moral people.

Our results also confirm findings by Smetana et al. (1999) indicating that hypothetical and actual transgressions are judged and justified differently. Personal narratives, by definition, are highly relevant to the self. Accordingly, reducing or eliminating cognitive inconsistencies or dissonance (cf. Festinger, 1957) by presenting oneself as a "good" person is aimed not only at others but also at oneself. Metaphorically, you would want to be able to look at yourself in the mirror without shuddering with horror or disgust at what you see (cf. Oscar Wilde's novel *The Picture of Dorian Gray*, where the beautiful but depraved Dorian senses that the more he sins, the uglier and more monstrous his painted portrait becomes). It seems that even young children strive to present themselves as morally good persons, thereby showing a basic understanding of what a moral audience expects of them.

References

Arsenio, W., Gold, J., & Adams, E. (2006). Children's conceptions and displays of moral emotions. In M. Killen & J. Smetana (Eds.), *Handbook of moral development* (pp. 581–609). Mahwah, NJ: Erlbaum.

Arsenio, W., & Lemerise, E. (2004). Aggression and moral development: Integrating social information processing and moral domain models. *Child Development, 75*, 987–1002.

Bretherton, I., Prentiss, C., & Ridgeway, D. (1990). Family relationships as represented in a story-completion task at thirty-seven and fifty-four months of age. *New Directions for Child Development, 48*, 85–105.

Bruner, J. (1990). *Acts of meaning*. Cambridge, MA: Harvard University Press.

Bruner, J. (2002). *Making stories: Law, literature, life*. New York: Farrar, Straus and Giroux.

Day, J. M. (1991). The moral audience: On the narrative mediation of moral "judgment" and moral "action." *New Directions for Child Development, 54*, 27–42.

Day, J. M., & Tappan, M. B. (1996). The narrative approach to moral development: From the epistemic subject to dialogical selves. *Human Development, 39*, 67–82.

De Vries, B., & Lehmann, A. J. (1996). The complexity of personal narratives. In J. E. Birren, G. M. Kenyon, J.-E. Ruth, J. J. Schroots, & T. Svensson (Eds.), *Aging and biography: Explorations in adult development* (pp. 149–166). New York: Springer.

Eisenberg, N. (2000). Emotion, regulation, and moral development. *Annual Review of Psychology, 51*, 665–697.

Ellsworth, P. C., & Scherer, K. R. (2003). Appraisal processes in emotion. In R. J. Davidson, K. R. Scherer, & H. H. Goldsmith (Eds.), *Handbook of the affective sciences* (pp. 572–595). New York/Oxford: Oxford University Press.

Emde, R. N., Wolf, D. P., & Oppenheim, D. (2003) (Eds.). *Revealing the inner worlds of young children. The Macarthur Story Stem Battery and parent-child narratives*. Oxford, UK: Oxford University Press.

Festinger, L. (1957). *A theory of cognitive dissonance*. Stanford, CA: Stanford University Press.

Flavell, J. H., Flavell, E. R., & Green, F. L. (2001). Development of children's understanding of connections between thinking and feeling. *Psychological Science, 12*, 430–432.

Gasser, L., & Keller, M. (2009). Are the competent the morally good? Perspective taking and moral motivation of children involved in bullying. *Social Development, 18*, 798–816.

Gergen, K., & Gergen, M. (1986). Narrative form and the construction of psychological science. In T. R. Sarbin (Ed.), *Narrative psychology. The storied nature of human conduct* (pp. 22–44). New York: Praeger.

Haidt, J. (2003). The moral emotions. In R. J. Davidson, K. R. Scherer, & H. H. Goldsmith (Eds.), *Handbook of affective sciences* (pp. 852–870). Oxford: Oxford University Press.

Hoffman, M. (2000). *Empathy and moral development: The implications for caring and justice*. Cambridge, UK: Cambridge University Press.

Hudson, J. A., & Shapiro, L. R. (1991). From knowing to telling: The development of children's scripts, stories, and personal narratives. In A. McCabe & C. Peterson (Eds.), *Developing narrative structure* (pp. 89–137). Hillsdale, NJ: Erlbaum.

Kochanska, G., Padavich, D. L., & Koenig, A. L. (1996). Children's narratives about hypothetical moral dilemmas and objective measures of their conscience: Mutual relations and socialization antecedents. *Child Development, 67*, 1420–1436.

Krettenauer, T., & Eichler, D. (2006). Adolescents' self-attributed emotions following a moral transgression: Relations with delinquency, confidence in moral judgment, and age. *British Journal of Developmental Psychology, 24*, 489–506.

Krettenauer, T., Malti, T., & Sokol, B. (2008). The development of moral emotion expectancies and the happy victimizer phenomenon: A critical review of theory and application. *European Journal of Developmental Science, 2*, 221–235.

Lourenço, O. (1997). Children's attributions of moral emotions to victimizers: Some data, doubts, and suggestions. *British Journal of Developmental Psychology, 15*, 425–438.

Malti, T., Gasser, L., & Buchmann, M. (2009). Aggressive and prosocial children's emotion attributions and moral reasoning. *Aggressive Behavior, 35*, 90–102.

Malti, T., Gasser, L., & Gutzwiller-Helfenfinger, E. (2010). Children's interpretive understanding, moral judgments, and emotion attributions: Relations to social behavior. *British Journal of Developmental Psychology*.

Malti, T., Gummerum, M., Keller, M., & Buchmann, M. (2009). Children's moral motivation, sympathy, and prosocial behavior. *Child Development, 80*, 442–460.

Malti, T., & Latzko, B. (2010). Children's moral emotions and moral cognition: Towards an integrative perspective. In B. Latzko & T. Malti (Eds.), *Children's moral emotions and moral cognition: Developmental and educational perspectives. New Directions for Child and Adolescent Development, 129*, 1–10.

Maxwell, B., & DesRoches, S. (2010). Empathy and social-emotional learning: Pitfalls and touchstones for school-based programs. In B. Latzko & T. Malti (Eds.), *Children's moral emotions and moral cognition: Developmental and educational perspectives. New Directions for Child and Adolescent Development, 129*, 33–53.

McAdams, D. P. (2008). Personal narratives and the life story. In O. P. John, R. W. Robins, & L. A. Pervin (Eds.), *Handbook of personality: Theory and research* (3rd ed., pp. 242–262). New York: Guilford Press.

Minnameier, G. (2010). The problem of moral motivation and the happy victimizer phenomenon: Killing two birds with one stone. In B. Latzko & T. Malti (Eds.), *Children's moral emotions and moral cognition: Developmental and educational perspectives. New Directions for Child and Adolescent Development, 129*, 55–75.

Narvaez, D. (2010). The emotional foundations of high moral intelligence. In B. Latzko & T. Malti (Eds.), *Children's moral emotions and moral cognition: Developmental and educational perspectives. New Directions for Child and Adolescent Development, 129*, 77–94.

Nicolopoulou, A. (1997). Children and narratives: Toward an interpretive and sociocultural approach. In M. Bamberg (Ed.), *Narrative development: Six approaches* (pp. 179–215). Mahwah, NJ: Erlbaum.

Nunner-Winkler, G. (2007). Development of moral motivation from childhood to early adulthood. *Journal of Moral Education, 36*, 399–414.

Packer, M. J. (1991). Interpreting stories, interpreting lives: Narrative and action in moral development research. *New Directions for Child Development, 54*, 63–82.

Piaget, J. (1967). *Biologie et connaissance* [Biology and awareness]. Paris. Gallimard.

Ramos-Marcuse, F., & Arsenio, W. F. (2001). Young children's emotionally-charged moral narratives: Relations with attachment and behavior problems. *Early Education & Development, 12*, 165–184.

Smetana, J. G., & Killen, M. (2008). Moral cognition, emotions, and neuroscience: An integrative developmental view. *European Journal of Developmental Science, 2*, 324–339.

Smetana, J. G., Schlagman, N., & Adams, P. (1993). Preschoolers' judgments about hypothetical and actual transgressions. *Child Development, 64*, 202–214.

Smetana, J. G., Toth, S. L., Cicchetti, D., Bruce, J., Kane, P., & Daddis, C. (1999). Maltreated and nonmaltreated preschoolers conceptions of hypothetical and actual moral transgressions. *Developmental Psychology, 35*, 269–281.

Tangney, J. P., Stuewig, J., & Mashek, D. J. (2007). Moral emotions and moral behavior. *Annual Review of Psychology, 58*, 345–372.

Tappan, M. B. (1991). Narrative, authorship, and the development of moral authority. *New Directions for Child Development, 54*, 5–25.

Tappan, M. B. (1998). Moral education in the zone of proximal development. *Journal of Moral Education, 27*, 141–160.

Tappan, M. B. (2006). Mediated moralities: Sociocultural approaches to moral development. In M. Killen & J. Smetana (Eds.), *Handbook of moral development* (pp. 351–374). Mahwah, NJ: Erlbaum.

Wainryb, C., Brehl, B. A., & Matwin, S. (2005). Being hurt and hurting others: Children's narrative accounts and moral judgments of their own interpersonal conflicts. *Monographs of the Society for Research in Child Development, 70*, 1–114.

Waldinger, R. J., Toth, S. L., & Gerber, A. (2001). Maltreatment and internal representation of relationships: Core relationship themes in the narratives of abused and neglected preschoolers. *Social Development, 10*, 42–58.

EVELINE GUTZWILLER-HELFENFINGER is professor of education and social sciences at the University of Teacher Education of Central Switzerland, Lucerne, Switzerland.

LUCIANO GASSER is an assistant professor at the University of Toronto Mississauga.

TINA MALTI is an assistant professor at the University of Toronto Mississauga.

Maxwell, B., & DesRoches, S. (2010). Empathy and social-emotional learning: Pitfalls and touchstones for school-based programs. In B. Latzko & T. Malti (Eds.), *Children's moral emotions and moral cognition: Developmental and educational perspectives. New Directions for Child and Adolescent Development*, *129*, 33–53. San Francisco: Jossey-Bass.

3

Empathy and Social-Emotional Learning: Pitfalls and Touchstones for School-Based Programs

Bruce Maxwell, Sarah DesRoches

Abstract

This chapter identifies three common pitfalls in the use of the concept of empathy in formal social-emotional learning interventions: (1) not distinguishing between affective and cognitive empathy ("equivocation"); (2) overestimating the role of the imagination in empathizing ("Piaget's fallacy"); and (3) not accommodating the developmental and psychological independence of affective and cognitive empathizing ("the fallacy of the Golden Rule"). Using case studies of existing programs, the chapter offers guidance on how to avoid these errors in program design. © Wiley Periodicals, Inc.

The authors acknowledge generous material support for this work from the following institutions: Institut de recherches cliniques de Montréal, Centre de recherche en éthique de l'Université de Montréal, Social Sciences and Humanities Research Council of Canada, and the Canadian Institutes of Health Research ("States of Mind" Network).

Psychological science can be a powerful reconstructive force in society when it is appropriately applied to the design of educational environments. Social-emotional learning programs grounded in developmental and social psychology are one means by which schools, charitable foundations, governments, and researchers attempt to realize the social values embedded in the specific developmental outcomes that such programs promote (Cahan, 2006). For instance, drawing on theoretical concepts from social information processing models of aggressive behavior (cf. Crick & Dodge, 1996), anti-violence programs such as Second Step (Duffel, Beland, & Frey, 2006), Responding in Peaceful and Positive Ways (Meyer, Farrell, Northup, Kung, & Plybon, 2001), and PeaceBuilders (Embry, Flannery, Vazsonyi, Powell, & Atha, 1996) seek to teach young people the social and emotional skills that are integral to a culture in which conflicts are resolved peacefully. In this way, these programs aim to promote human values such as peace, order, and stability. Similarly, research on mutual recognition in children's identity development (cf. Honig, Leu, & Nissen, 1996) provides the theoretical frame for Kinderwelten, an anti-bias program that explicitly aims to integrate the values of inclusion, equality, human diversity, and fairness into the practices and daily routines of early child-care centers (Krause, Şıkcan, & Wagner, 2004).

Schools have many different social-emotional learning programs to choose from. But how does a school decide which program will be most effective in helping it achieve its particular normative aims? How can educational decision makers ensure that a particular program is worth the significant investment of time, money, and energy required to implement and maintain it?

Too often, program evaluation is the sole watchword for the question of "what works" in social development interventions (cf. Tolan & Guerra, 1994). Flannery and colleagues' plea that the methods of psychological science be put into service of violence prevention in society typifies this perspective. "If psychologists are to inform public policy and facilitate risk prevention for young people," they write, "it is imperative that we identify, through applied evaluation studies, programs that effectively prevent youth violent behavior and its associated precursors (i.e., aggression) and rigorously evaluate the behavioral outcomes associated with these interventions" (Flannery et al., 2003, p. 293). This approach has limitations. Program evaluation is, at best, one piece of the puzzle. Another equally valuable piece is the epidemiological perspective: the extent to which a program takes into consideration the complex social-contextual explanations of youth violence. Still another is the perspective of psychological theory: the extent to which a program is well designed using valid theoretical constructs and models in psychology.

Regarding the issue of theoretical drivenness in violence prevention programs, Tolan and Guerra (1994) offer a discouraging generalization about the experimental designs of social-learning interventions. Most programs, they point out, are led by concerns about how well content coheres with curricular frameworks or how easily it can be integrated into ongoing classes. Sometimes violence prevention programs are merely off-label uses of programs created to address other social problems. A shortage of a posteriori empirical data on program efficacy is not the only reason to doubt such approaches to program design. The other is that, by lacking a theoretical base in psychological science, there is no a priori psychological reason to believe that they might be effective in reducing youth violence either. Youth violence, we are told, is a significant public health problem (U.S. Department of Health and Human Services [USDHHS], 2001). More than any other sector of the population, moreover, it is the young people who engage in violent behavior themselves who are affected by violence most (USDHHS, 2001). In this context, the implementation of programs whose effects are unknown and have no psychological basis seems to amount to pottering about in young people's lives and with matters that are of the utmost social consequence. And to this extent, there is ample room to question whether such interventions meet acceptable standards of educational ethics.

For the sake of advancing the cause of theoretically grounded social-emotional learning programs, this chapter identifies three misconceptualizations of the relationship between moral emotions and moral cognition that recur in such programs. Focusing on one moral emotion that is especially salient in violence prevention and anti-bias programs—namely, empathy—our approach is to present salient empirical findings and conceptual considerations that help us both understand what these "pitfalls" (as we call them) are and how to avoid making them. We refer to these correctives as "touchstones": key points on the meaning and psychology of "empathy," "empathizing," and the allied concepts of "perspective taking" and "social inferencing" that are meant to signpost ways to avoid these errors in the design of social-emotional learning interventions. The first pitfall is failing to distinguish between empathy as a feeling of concern for others (i.e., "affective empathy") from empathy as simply awareness of other people's experiences—their feelings, desires, beliefs, intentions, etc. (i.e., "cognitive empathy"). We label this pitfall "equivocation." To most people, the word "empathy" suggests an emotion closely related to compassion or sympathy. Thus, when a program offers activities that are appropriate for learning skills important to cognitive empathy but claims that these activities support "empathy," the programs' intended outcomes become confusing. The second pitfall is overestimating the role of the imagination in empathizing. By "imagination" we mean the mental act of placing oneself vicariously in another person's position, a cognitively demanding psychological process that psychologists usually referred to as "perspective taking." The typical effect on program design of "Piaget's fallacy" (as we will call it) is that imagination comes to be featured as a core learning area and literature is prioritized as a program medium. When interventions overestimate the need for imagination, they place an unnecessary obstacle between the young people in the program and the experiences of empathizing with others that such programs often try to facilitate. The third pitfall, the so-called "fallacy of the Golden Rule," is characterized by failing to appreciate that cognitive empathizing and affective empathizing are developmentally and psychologically independent social skills. The most prevalent and important of the three design pitfalls in social-emotional learning interventions discussed in this chapter, the fallacy of the Golden Rule has two main manifestations. Its first manifestation is the doubtful assumption that teaching skills in understanding others' emotions and experiences is, on its own, a means to encouraging empathy as a personal trait. As Narvaez points out in Chapter Five of this volume, moral expertise (or empathy) requires, "a holistic and contextualized understanding that engages the entire brain-mind-body system." Applicable only to programs targeting preschool-aged children, the fallacy of the Golden Rule's second manifestation is the failure to include measures to support young children's empathic development through direct adult socialization.

Equivocation: Disambiguating "Empathy"

The disambiguation of "empathy" begins by appreciating that the term designates two distinct psychological phenomena: (1) insight into another's thoughts, beliefs, desires, intentions, or emotions (i.e., "cognitive empathy"); and (2) unpleasant emotional reactions to the perception of another's suffering, misfortune, or distress (i.e., "affective empathy").

Moral psychologists whose research is in the constructivist paradigm of Piaget and Kohlberg tend to understand empathy primarily in the sense of cognitive empathy. "Perspective taking," as cognitive empathy is usually called in this research tradition, is an enabling mental capacity that serves reflection on social conflicts from a point of view other than the child's own. Moral development traces a process of cognitive decentration particular to the social domain (Turiel, 1998). At the beginning of this process, children have an egocentric view of social problems. The perspective of egocentrism, from which they can only consider their own point of view, gradually gives way to one which is attentive to multiple features of the situation, and which includes the ability to coordinate those features (Flavell, Miller, & Miller, 2002). Part of what is "constructed" in cognitive moral development, then, is this broader, more differentiated social attention. As described starkly by Martin Hoffman (2000), "cognitive development enables children to [...] free themselves from the grip of their own perspective, and to take another's perspective as well" (p. 160). In this way, an increased propensity to empathize is regarded in the cognitive developmental tradition as a key to adequately grasping the point of a valid moral norm—namely, the promotion of individual rights, equal regard for welfare, and justice (Gibbs, 2003).

When psychologists conceive of empathy in the second, affective sense, they are led to regard empathy as a state of emotional involvement that can motivate pro-social behavior. In this view, empathizing means being troubled by threats to others' well being and often being moved to alleviate those threats. Ethicists and laypeople alike tend to adopt a similar usage: "empathy" primarily refers to "involvement in another's suffering as something to be relieved" (Nagel, 1970, p. 80). In ordinary language, then, "empathy" is synonymous with "sympathy" or "compassion." Although ethicists usually associate empathizing with helping, pro-social, and moral behavior, social psychologists are more reserved. For methodological reasons, the latter typically define empathy merely as *distress* felt in response to the perception of another's adversity. A central project of empathy research in social psychology historically has been to scrutinize the popular notion that empathy is a "moral emotion" insofar as it motivates people to help others. However, the inclusion of a desire to help, within the definition of the construct under investigation, risks begging, in effect, the very research question to be resolved.

That said, empathy research in social psychology has ended up corroborating the assumption of folk-psychology that empathic distress amplifies motivation to act pro-socially. In ageing reviews of this large body of empirical literature going back over thirty years, Martin Hoffman (2000) and Daniel Batson (1991) independently conclude that feelings of empathy for a person in need increase the likelihood that the empathizer will respond by helping to relieve that need. In light of these findings, Miller and colleagues conclude that responding pro-socially to others' distress belongs in the definition of empathy (Miller, Eisenberg, Fabes, & Shell, 1996).

Avoiding Equivocation in Program Design. Unsurprisingly, the terminological inconsistency that surrounds "empathy" is reflected in discrepant conceptualizations of the construct in anti-violence and anti-bias programs. For instance, in the Kinderwelten program "deliberately seek[s] to cultivate and teach this trait to young students," one can infer from the context that the trait in question is affective empathy. A hallmark of Kinderwelten is the classroom visit by a so-called Persona doll, a life-sized educator-operated puppet who tells the children personal stories about having been teased or excluded because of superficial differences (name, skin or hair color, style of speech or dress, etc.). The rationale for using these dolls, the documentation explains, is "to encourage empathy for what the dolls may have experienced as a result of their unfair treatment" (Krause, Şıkcan, & Wagner, 2004). By contrast, the operative definition of "empathy" in the Second Step violence-prevention program is empathy as social inferencing, or "cognitive empathy." According to this program's literature, empathy is the broad social competency of knowing what other people are thinking and understanding why they are thinking it. So conceived, empathy includes "knowledge of the emotions of self and others," "perspective taking," "vicariously experiencing others' feelings," and "responding emotionally to others" (Committee for Children, 2002, p. 2). Taken out of context, this last dimension of empathy is easily misread as an attempt to encompass compassionate empathy. Rather, Second Step considers "responding to others" as a specific skill of communicating one's emotional reactions to one's perceptions of others not a specific disposition to respond with personal concern to others in states of adversity (Duffel, Beland, & Frey, 2006).

As long as such *intra*-program consistency in the use of "empathy" pertains, perhaps *inter*-program ambiguity is tolerable? Indeed, program designers are entitled to stipulate within reasonable limits the definition of core constructs. Besides, there are parallel histories in the social sciences that comprehend empathy as modes of introspection, which are, respectively, value-neutral and value-laden (Maxwell, 2008). In our view, there is one good and simple reason why a social development program should align itself with the tradition of conceiving empathy in the affective sense: Calling social inferencing "empathy" is confusing. Clearly, the insight into other people's perspectives that social inferencing affords may be used for harmful, deceitful, or malicious ends. Wishing to make a victim of a classmate, a victimizer may call the child a nickname that she knows the child finds especially hurtful. This is a case where the victimizer empathizes with the child to more effectively harm her. To pre-psychological ears, of course, that sentence just sounds wrong. Thus, when social-development interventions use "empathy" to mean social inferencing they run the risk of misleading their constituency—educators, children, parents, and possibly even themselves—into believing that structured activities that improve empathy skills foster affective empathy. We recommend adding a layer of complexity to our language by speaking in the following way: Structured activities that improve social inferencing skills foster *as a matter of course* empathy as a disposition of personal concern for others' well-being. (Whether or not this is a legitimate assumption is a question we return to in the third substantive section of this chapter.) For now, we turn in the next section to the developmentally, functionally, and conceptually complex relationship between cognitive empathy and affective empathy. Educators will be better positioned to effectively support the growth of the key social capacities of empathizing and social inferencing when they appreciate this relationship and find ways of working with it. One crucial way that social-development interventions can begin to do this is by adopting a vocabulary that opposes and resists, rather than contributes to and reinforces, the confusing tendency in folk moral psychology to equivocate between the affective and conceptions of empathy. That means being careful not to refer to social inferencing as "empathy."

Piaget's Fallacy: Equating Perspective Taking with Cognitive Empathy

Empathizing may involve perspective taking, but perspective taking does not necessarily involve concern for others. The statement describes two aspects of the vexing relationship between perspective taking and empathizing. The first is that a person may experience other-directed concern without perspective taking. Perspective taking, that is to say, is not *necessary* for empathy. The second is that it is not *sufficient* either. In other words, it is possible for a person to become imaginatively involved in another's aversive situation without experiencing personal distress (i.e., "affective empathy") for the sufferer. This section considers the first of these points. The following section addresses the second.

Grasping the first point—namely, that empathizing does not imply perspective taking—requires us to liberate ourselves from a piece of constraining usage inherited from the Piagetian tradition in cognitive psychology. Cognitive empathizing (i.e., "social inferencing"), as we described it in the last section, is the capacity humans have to formulate beliefs about others' inner states, to infer what is sometimes called a "theory of mind" from situational cues. One common way of understanding "perspective taking" is to define it in reference to one particular psychological process by which it is thought that people acquire beliefs about others' inner states—namely, by imagining oneself in that other person's experience. When perspective taking is conceived in this way, the assumption is that human beings' primary route of access to others' beliefs, desires, intentions, and so on, is via the imagination. To adapt Endel Tulving's (1985) expression, it is thought that we come to understand others' perspectives, that is, by engaging in a more-or-less effortful act of "intersubjective mental travel." Let us call this "the imaginative conception of social inferencing."

The imaginative conception of social inferencing has a long pedigree in philosophical ethics. "We have no immediate experience of what other men feel, we can form no idea of the manner in which they are affected," Adam Smith famously postulated, "but by conceiving what we ourselves should feel in the situation" 1759/2009, p. 8) and described empathy (he called it "sympathy") as "changing places in fancy with the sufferer." The failure to distinguish between the imaginative *processes* assumed to be involved in cognitive empathy and the epistemological *aims* of perspective taking also frequently occurs in treatments of empathy in contemporary psychology. A number of commentators attribute the pervasiveness of the imaginative conception of social inferencing in psychology to the fact that Piaget used a visual perspective-taking task (i.e., his famous Three Mountain Task) in his early experiments on theory of mind (cf. Davis, 1994; Eisenberg, Murphy, & Shepard, 1997; Higgins, 1981). Be that as it may, it is itself psychological research on the mechanisms involved in social inferencing that belies it. It turns out that "perspective taking" understood as imagining oneself in another's situation is just one of several different psychological mechanisms that can mediate empathic distress.

What, then, are the other mechanisms? The several reviews of the psychological literature on this topic show that empathic arousal can be cognitively much simpler than the imaginative conception of perspective taking supposes. However, in so far as empathizing can draw on a diverse assortment of distinguishable psychological processes, the overall story of empathic arousal is more complex (for reviews see Davis, 1994; Hoffman, 2000). The range of psychological processes that can mediate experience of empathic distress divides into two categories: reactive and introspective modes (Maxwell, 2008). The first, more cognitively simple modes, embrace responses to particular features of the object of empathy. These include (1) "conditioning," where visual cues such as the sight of blood elicit distressing feelings; (2) "mimicry," where the involuntary imitation of a person in distress produces feelings in the imitator that affectively match those of the imitated; (3) "direct association," a process whereby feelings of compassion are triggered via the association either of a particular feature of another person's experience of suffering or his or her situation (usually with some traumatic or distressing event in the observer's own past). The second category, the more cognitively complex "introspective" modes, includes social-inferencing mechanisms—that is, mechanisms used directly to obtain information about others' mental states. These are (a) "language-mediated association," which refers to a very broad set of situations. In Chapter Two of this volume, Gutzwiller-Helfenfinger, Gasser, and Malti provide an example in which language plays a central role in communicating a person's feelings or her empathy-evoking situation by exploring how children make sense of moral issues through narrative; (b) "labeling," or drawing inferences about another's internal states from standard social beliefs or generalizations about personality types; (c) "cognitive networking" where inferences about a person's inner states are drawn from stereotyped chunks of knowledge about perceptual cues (especially social scripts); and finally (7) "perspective taking" which, again, refers narrowly in this context to strictly imagination-mediated other-directed introspection. Perspective taking, furthermore, can take two forms. Self-focused perspective taking is imagining how one would feel or react if one were oneself in another's aversive situation. Self-focused perspective taking, by contrast, is imagining what it would be like to be a person believed to be in an aversive state.

For the purposes of this chapter, the catalogue of psychological processes involved in empathizing is instructive primarily because it exposes the imaginative conception of perspective taking as a received idea. What turns out to be wrong with this conception is that it presupposes, incorrectly, that effective social inferencing depends on cognitively demanding imaginative psychological processes. For the sake of keeping this distinction straight, it may help to rigorously reserve the term "perspective taking" to refer exclusively to imagination-mediated introspection—that is what Adam Smith (1759/2009) called "changing places in the fancy with the sufferer," what Kohut (1959) called "vicarious introspection," and what we called above "intersubjective travel"—and to avoid using it to refer generically to social inferencing.

Novels as Education for Compassionate Citizenry: A Case Study. An example of the influence of the imaginative conception of social inferencing on the design of a social-development intervention can be found in some of Martha Nussbaum's writings on citizenship education (cf. Nussbaum, 1995, 2001). Nussbaum's idea is that empathy (she calls it "compassion") is essential to good citizenship. In her view, it plays not only a moral-perceptive role in helping citizens see that *there are* certain basic personal and social capacities which are necessary for human well-being. Empathy also plays a moral-motivational role by enabling cocitizens to *appreciate that they owe each other* the provision and protection of those basic capacities. The study of realist social novels is the centerpiece of Nussbaum's proposal about how formal education can foster such bonds of social solidarity. Her reason for prioritizing literature in this regard is plain: No other form of expression has as much potential to develop the ability to perspective take, to imagine oneself in another person's position (she calls this ability "empathy"). Indeed, Nussbaum remarks that even when literature lacks explicit political content, it still serves a "vital political function" because it cultivates perspective taking, an imaginative ability she considers central to political life (2001, p. 433).

The assumption of the imaginative conception of social inferencing (i.e., overlooking the multifacetedness of empathic arousal) manifests itself in Nussbaum's proposal by imposing artificial barriers to the intervention's own success. Its purpose is to stimulate appropriate feelings of empathy towards certain groups of cocitizens with whom participants might otherwise have trouble identifying. However, it is important to notice the fallout limitations from assuming the imaginative conception of social inferencing. Because this assumption pictures "imagination" as the sine qua non of empathizing, it makes the inclusion of support for cognitively advanced perspective taking as a psycho-social soft skill appear essential. It determines the selection of literature as its medium. It also, incidentally, casts childhood as a period of empathic latency; in Nussbaum's eyes, the improvement of perspective taking abilities occurs through childhood, but children will not be able empathize until they have achieved a certain sophistication in the use of their imaginative faculties (2001, pp. 426–428). If seeking to improve perspective taking competency seems unobjectionable, and the denial of children's ability to empathize simply uninformed, the restrictive use of a single, cognitively demanding medium is more worrisome. Especially for participants with weak perspective-taking skills, the use of literature constitutes an arbitrary impediment to those participants' potential for achieving the program's goals. Yet there is a simple solution to this problem: privilege a less cognitively demanding medium (e.g., film), or better, employ a range of media that reflect the psychological diversity of empathic arousal.

Martin Hoffman (2000), it may be said, regarded the many modes of empathic arousal as part of human beings' empathic "hardware." Both primitive and more cognitively advanced arousal mechanisms are typically operational and mutually supporting in any particular experience of compassionate empathy. In this way, the multifacetedness of empathic arousal virtually compels a caring response on the part of a bystander to a person in distress. But Hoffman (2000) did not regard human beings as "saintly empathic-distress-leads-to-helping machines" (p. 33). These two assertions are consistent as long as we take care, as Hoffman did, to keep social inferencing and the psychological processes involved in the *awareness* that someone is suffering adversity well distinct from the responding emotionally to that suffering by *caring*. It is, of course, possible and even commonplace to perceive another's suffering otherwise—for instance, a case of chronic pain as a professional problem to be solved, or as in the emotion *Schadenfreude*, a detested politician getting embroiled in an embarrassing scandal as cause for satisfied amusement. And, as it often the case, one may simply be indifferent. As we will point out in the next section, not all developmental psychologists and social-intervention program designers have been as careful as Hoffman.

The Fallacy of the Golden Rule: Social Inferencing Leads to Caring

Similar to the idea that empathic distress amplifies motivation to act prosocially presented above, the notion that the perception of suffering typically leads to empathizing seems to be widespread in moral folk psychology. In Chapter Four of this volume, Minnameier outlines a similar concept, that of the "happy victimizer" in which children are aware of moral rules but break them to serve their own interest. These errors underwrite, for instance, the common discipline encounter in which an adult attempts to stimulate transgressor guilt in a victimizer by exhorting the child to "imagine how you would feel!"—that is, to perspective take with an actual or potential victim (Maxwell & Reichenbach 2007). It is also featured in Daniel Goleman's bellwether book *Emotional Intelligence* (1995) and, in particular, in the case Goleman makes for why "empathy is the core of social competence." "Empathy leads to caring, altruism, and compassion. Seeing things from another's perspective breaks down biased stereotypes, and thus breeds tolerance and acceptance of differences. These capacities are ever-more called on in our increasingly pluralistic society, allowing people to live together in mutual respects" (p. 285), Goleman argues. The assumption has been labeled "the fallacy of the Golden Rule" on the grounds that it is a supposition of its eponymous moral rule of thumb (Maxwell, 2008). Thoughts about, "what you would not have done unto you," have motivational currency only to the extent that the imaginer cares about what is "done unto others," that she regards others as being worthy of the same respectful attention she believes she merits herself. This section considers the developmental significance of the psychological independence of empathy and social inferencing by reviewing salient points of Hoffman's critique of Kohlberg's theory of cognitive moral development.

Hoffman's Critique of Kohlberg. Hoffman (2000), like many other critics of Kohlberg's theory (cf. Kohlberg, 1981, 1984) held that the Piagetian tradition in cognitive moral development research has trouble explaining moral motives and moral engagement. He takes no objection to the paradigmatic assumption that the process that underlies *cognitive* moral development is decentration. This shift, described above, is from a style of social deliberation based on the child's own egocentric perspective towards an ideal of impartial judgment where the perspectives of all stakeholders in a social conflict are coordinated (cf. Gibbs, 2003). Rather, the Piagetian framework, in Hoffman's view, is limited because it contains no theoretical resources to explain why perspective taking should serve pro-social rather than egoistic ends. Otherwise stated, what is absent in cognitive moral developmentalism is an account of why, in Hoffman's words, "the knowledge of others' perspectives that is gained in the context of conflicting claims [should] lead children to take others' claims seriously and be willing to negotiate and compromise their own claims, rather than use the knowledge to manipulate the other" (2000, p. 131). Having beliefs about another's state of adversity may be a *necessary* condition of having feelings of solidaristic caring towards that individual, but it is not sufficient. By failing to accommodate empathic development as something distinct from decentration in the social domain, cognitive moral developmentalism, in sum, commits the fallacy of the Golden Rule.

The distinction between perspective taking and empathizing "throws down the gauntlet" to child development researchers to elucidate educationally informative differences between the development of the capacity for perspective taking and empathic development. Hoffman himself was not slow in picking it up. Completing and complementing Kohlberg's theory by filling the explanatory gap he had exposed was for Hoffman one of the main purposes of theory and research in empathic development. One of Hoffman's most important contributions to knowledge in developmental psychology was to advance and then to build an empirical case for two touchstones that are of enormous practical import for intervention in children's social development: that empathic development is (1) relatively precocious, and (2) requires adult intervention.

Precocity. The precocity of empathic development means that, relative to cognitive moral development, the main achievements of empathic development occur in early childhood (Hoffman, 2000). When tertiary cognitive abilities begin to arrive in late childhood they start to work in conjunction with an already established disposition to respond with concern to others' distress. This enables the kind of abstract and complex empathizing characteristic of deliberation over practical moral problems (Gibbs, 2003; Hoffman, 2000).

Hastings, Zahn-Waxler, Robinson, Usher, and Bridges (2000) research has helped refine Hoffman's claim about the precocity of empathic development by providing evidence for a sensitive period. Studying the way that children with significant behavior problems (e.g., frequent aggressiveness) respond when they witness harm to others, the researchers observed that children with behavior problems at age four showed about the same level of personal concern as children without behavior problems. Aggressive children may lack impulse control, that is, but not empathy. By age seven, however, the picture has changed significantly. At this age, while children with no previous behavior problems showed increased responses of concern for persons who are hurt or upset, the empathic responsiveness of children with behavior problems has now decreased. Between four and seven, it seems, is a crucial period for empathic development. It is then where at-risk children appear to drop away from their peers in terms of making age-expectant gains in personal concern.

Socialization Dependence. Another touchstone of empathic development that we can partly credit to Hoffman is the claim that empathic development depends on adult intervention. This position sets Hoffman in direct opposition to Piagetian constructivism, a broad doctrine in developmental psychology, which, among other things, minimized the significance of structured, adult-led learning environments for social and cognitive development and emphasizes instead free, child-led interaction and dialogue between peers. Anticipating current prevailing theorizing in evolutionary biology (cf. Bloom, 2004), Hoffman thought that humans have a biologically rooted adaptive disposition towards concern for others or "empathy" (Hoffman, 1981). Yet, as already mentioned above, a moment's reflection on the histories of human interaction confirms that humans are no saintly pro-social machines. A successful outcome in empathic development is by no means biologically guaranteed. Is there a tension here that needs to be reconciled? Scrupulously avoiding the fallacy of the Golden rule, Hoffman distinguishes between a biological aversion to human suffering, empathy as a "moral emotion" if you will, from a decentered awareness of the potentially harmful consequences of one's actions towards others. It is the former that must be taught by adults and learned by children.

The ability to empathize does not make people altruists, but it does enable them to be trained out of systematically prioritizing their interests in conflicts with those of others, Hoffman concluded. Social conflicts are typically conflicts between competing personal interests or "egoistic desires" (for social dominance, safety, material advantages, etc.). Hoffman's reasoning is that, in such situations, first-person interests desensitize people's intuitions to the harms to others implied by conflict outcomes and can fuel post hoc rationalizations for resolutions that would serve those interests. "Even highly empathic children can get emotionally involved when pursuing their goals or when their desires conflict with others" (p. 169), he says. So, if an empathic disposition does not make people impartial, it nevertheless serves impartiality indirectly by making people "receptive to environments that can make them aware of the consequences of their actions" (p. 169).

The role adults can play is crucial in moral socialization. Far from being spontaneously constructed by children in the course of free peer interaction à la Piaget (cf. Piaget, 1932; Kohlberg, 1984), an interest in morality has to be "induced" in early childhood. Induction, in Hoffman's sense, is an umbrella term for discipline encounters in which an adult, in reaction to a violent transgression on a child's part, tries to stimulate a sense of conscience (i.e., "guilty feelings") by drawing attention to the nature of the harm and to the fact that the child is responsible for the harm. In this way, Hoffman (2000) writes, induction makes "the connection, necessary for guilt and moral internalization, between children's egoistic motives, their behavior, and their behavior's harmful consequences for others" (p. 142). Many parents and caregivers use induction pretheoretically of course, without any prior training or instruction. Ostensibly, they do this because they believe that induction serves the interests of cooperative and pro-social behavior, on which the stability and flourishing of human society depends. Because it is through induction that children acquire a habituated disposition to control their behavior out of consideration for others that induction is, for Hoffman (2000), the most important for moral development of all the discipline encounters that can occur between children and adults (p. 142).

In this connection, we have again a significant point of departure from the Kohlbergian paradigm—and one that, incidentally, casts Hoffman as something of an adherent to a dual-processing model of moral cognition *avant la lettre* (for a review of these models see Lapsley & Hill, 2008). Whereas in the Kohlbergian paradigm, fairness and altruistic caring depend on the intervention of explicit, consciously accessible cognitive moral structures or "reasons" to hold in check unreflective egoistic inclinations, in Hoffman's model, the latter are regulated by a socialized affective disposition that is itself intuitive: automatic, quick, and not readily accessible to consciousness. Relevant studies on parenting style and pro-social behavior largely validate the key postulate of Hoffman's theory of moral socialization—namely, that induction and pro-social behavior in children is mediated by children's empathy (for a review, see Gibbs, 2003, pp. 103–105).

Teaching "Emotional Understanding" in Second Step for Preschoolers: A Case Study. Second Step is a violence-prevention program based on the social and emotional learning research program in positive psychology (Duffel et al., 2006). A central theoretical claim of the program is that a lack of social-emotional skills is an important contributor to aggressive behavior. Second Step is not, however, a "selective" prevention program. That is, it is not designed for use with children who have already demonstrated violent behavior or who are at risk for engaging in it. Consistent with the general orientation of positive psychology, the program documentation emphasizes that strong social-emotional skills are predictors of various markers of social success—peer acceptance, academic performance, pro-social behavior, better general social skills, etc. (cf. Seligman & Csikszentmihalyi, 2000). All children, then, can benefit from social and emotional learning. By targeting all children within a certain population in this way, Second Step falls into the category of "universal" prevention programs.

The purpose of Second Step is to complement the positive social and emotional learning that may occur in homes by teaching social-emotional competencies in the formal learning environment of the school. Its lessons and activities are designed around four key areas: "social problems solving," "emotion management," "behavioral skills," and "empathy" (Committee for Children, 2002). The "empathy" component is, in turn, broken down into four teachable skill areas: accurately identifying emotions and their expression, social inferencing (the program documentation refers to it as "perspective taking"), vicariously experiencing emotions that are more congruent with another's situation than with one's own (i.e., feeling happy or sad "with" or "for" another person), and communicating one's own emotions effectively (Committee for Children, 2002).

The empathy unit, designed for use with children at the preschool/kindergarten level, focuses on "identifying feelings in self and others" (this skill area is also referred to as "emotional understanding"). The program summary prepared by the Committee for Children (2002) cites research by Izard, Fine, Schultz, Mostow, and Ackerman (2001) on the significance of emotional-understanding skills at preschool/kindergarten age (i.e., five years) as a predictor of academic success at the level of grades four and five (i.e., nine years) as justification for this orientation. Photo-lesson cards are the centerpiece of teaching emotional understanding. The cards illustrate seven putatively universal human emotions: happy, sad, angry, surprised, scared, disgusted, and worried. By examining pictures of people experiencing these emotions, children are meant to learn how to better identify these emotions' physiological characteristics. Educators are also invited to use the cards as a starting point for role-playing activities in which children practice physically displaying these emotions and detecting them in others.

Emotional understanding, in the sense it is understood in the Second Step program, may well contribute to social and academic success, and using photo cards may be an effective way to teach emotional understanding. The question we wish to consider, however, is how adequate is teaching emotional understanding as a means of supporting empathy and the empathic development of young children? In light of this section's discussion of the conceptual and developmental distinction between social inferencing and concern for others, the answer is not far to seek. If empathic development depends on inductive practices on the part of adults, Second Step seems to commit the fallacy of the Golden Rule. It reiterates, in other words, the Kohlbergian presumption that, by looking after social inferencing, concern for others will look after itself.

This critique is open to an objection: that empathy (i.e., the personal disposition to be concerned for others) is not actually one of Second Step's outcome goals. On one hand, Second Step tends to employ the term "empathy" in the cognitive sense, as we pointed out above in the first section. Hence, in the program's terms, teaching in the skill area of "empathy" coextends with teaching in the skill area of social inferencing. On the other hand, some of Second Step's program documentation points in another direction. For example, Daniel Goleman's conception of empathy is sometimes cited as the source of the program's four-part definition of empathy. And, as we saw earlier too, Goleman (1995) vaunts "empathy" (i.e., "social inferencing") as no less than the key social competency precisely because it is conducive to "caring," "altruism," "compassion," "tolerance," acceptance of difference," and "mutual respect" (p. 285). Should we conclude that the rationale behind "empathy lessons" in Second Step is to contribute to children's later success at work and school *irrespective of* whether empathy as a personal trait is important to social adaptation? Or, are we meant to understand that the social-emotional skills involved in social inferencing contribute to children's later success at work and school *because* these skills are conducive to empathy as a personal trait? There seems to be a genuine ambiguity in Second Step about what it seeks to achieve by teaching empathy.

In either case, the program's handling of this key construct seems problematic. If "empathy" is intended to be synonymous with "social inferencing" then, this usage is an important impediment to seeing for what they really are the program's goals vis-à-vis empathy. As mentioned above in the section on equivocation, in the ears of a general audience, "empathy" connotes caring; not just knowing what another person is experiencing, but a pro-social awareness of another person's suffering. On the other hand, if emotional understanding skills are a program goal because they are ancillary to the emergence of empathy as a personal trait, then social inferencing lessons *alone* are inadequate to the task. There are substantial grounds for believing that empathy is a socialized disposition and that the preschool/kindergarten age is a critical period for developing empathy. Taking empathic development seriously in social interventions targeting this age group means making some accommodation for empathic socialization. Its absence in Second Step thus appears to be an important design flaw.

The inclusion of inductive practices as part of an intervention in social development may strike some educators as being an illegitimate manipulation of children's emotions—if not a clear violation of parents' rights to raise their children according to their own values. Even if empathic development does require adult intervention, perhaps it is more appropriate to leave this particular task to family members in the intimate context of the home. From this perspective, the focus of Second Step on emotional understanding looks justified on *ethical* grounds. To this objection, we would reply that leaving empathic socialization to the hazards of socialization in this way leaves at risk the very children who stand to benefit most from a school-based anti-violence program. Because, as noted above, induction is widespread "pre-psychological" parenting practice, educators can be confident that many of the children they work with will be receiving adequate informal developmental support. Yet those who are not are at the greatest risk for future behavior problems. Again, recognizing the extent to which social inferencing skills are psychologically independent from others helps us to appreciate that teaching emotional understanding is no substitute for support for empathic development. The point is brought home forcefully by the results of research on the use of "perspective taking training" in the treatment of psychopathic criminals. The overall picture of the various investigations into the re-offending of psychopaths who followed a treatment program is that treatment, and especially social skills and social perspective-taking treatment programs, do not lead to a decrease, but astonishingly, rather to an increase of criminal behavior (D'Silva, Dugan, & McCarthy, 2004). Assuming, with Rice, Harris, and Cormier (1992), that the empathy-training programs did in fact succeed in improving offenders' perspective-taking abilities, this experience suggests, again, that when perspective taking is psychologically divorced from Hoffmanian empathic disposition of concern for others, knowledge gained through perspective taking contributes little to the motivation of moral behavior (Table 3.1).

Conclusion

Drawing on established research findings in social and developmental psychology, this chapter outlined three pitfalls in the use of "empathy," "perspective taking," and allied psychological concepts in school-based interventions in social-emotional learning. It also sought to sketch a set of touchstones for avoiding these errors in program design and documentation. Following the example of Kinderwelten, programs can avoid the confusion about program goals that equivocation engenders by using the

Table 3.1. Pitfalls and Touchstones on Empathy, Perspective Taking, and Allied Concepts in the Design of Social-Emotional Learning Programs

Pitfall	*Corrective*	*Touchstones*
Equivocation: Conflating "empathy's" two senses	The term "empathy" designates two main psychological phenomena: social inferencing ("cognitive" empathy) and concern for others ("affective" empathy).	(a) Use the term "empathy" only to refer to affective empathy. (b) Avoid using the term "empathy" to refer to cognitive empathy. (c) Use the term "social inferencing" to refer to cognitive empathy instead.
Piaget's fallacy: Empathizing always involves imagining oneself in a sufferer's experience	Perspective taking ("imagining oneself in another's experience") is but one of several psychological mechanisms that mediate empathy.	(a) Use the term "perspective taking" only to refer to imaginative introspection. (b) Avoid using the term "perspective taking" to refer to social inferencing (c) Benefit from the multifacetedness of empathic arousal by using a range of media (stories, personal encounters, images, etc.).
Fallacy of the Golden Rule: Awareness of another's adversity leads to empathizing	Empathy is but one of many ways to be involved in another's adversity: as a technical problem to be solved, as cause for satisfied amusement ("Schadenfreude"), etc. Indifference is also a psychologically possible reaction to others' suffering. Empathy is a socialized disposition of other-directed concern whose development requires support from adult intervention.	(a) Supporting social inferencing skills is not ipso facto a means of nurturing concern for others. (b) Inductive strategies should be included and facilitators informed about empathy socialization. (c) The target population of empathic-development interventions should be preschool-aged children.

term "social inferencing" (rather than "empathy") to refer to cognitive empathy and using "empathy" only to refer to affective empathy. Learning a lesson from Nussbaum's proposal to put the study of social realist novels at the center of citizenship education, programs can avoid unnecessary dependence on cognitively demanding, imagination-heavy media. Once unbound by Piaget's fallacy, the multifacetedness of empathic arousal becomes a resource. Programs are free to avail themselves of the full scope of media as tools for encouraging empathic understanding of others in situations of adversity. Finally, the fallacy of the Golden Rule, illustrated in the discussion of Second Step, can be avoided by finding ways to accommodate the basics of what is known in psychology about the different developmental trajectories of empathy and social inferencing. A good place to start, in this connection, is not to take for granted that activities that strengthen social inferencing skills will also nurture empathizing. Because preschool age is a crucial time for empathic development, preschoolers whose empathic development is compromised in their home environments have the most to gain from the social-emotional learning interventions. By prioritizing inductive strategies, and especially by outreach to permanent school staff, programs can maximize their chances of having a significant positive impact on these children's lives.

Although this study's primary aim has been to constructively criticize questionable conceptualizations of "empathy" that are abroad in social-emotional learning programs, its wider significance is to serve as a reminder of the tenuous relationship between research and practice in moral education, on one hand, and folk conceptions of moral functioning, on the other. Quivocation between affective and cognitive empathy, Piaget's fallacy, and the fallacy of Golden Rule are three widespread received ideas about the relationship between moral emotions and moral cognition. All three pitfalls are maintained and partly explained by the same tendency in folk psychology to infer from the plausible claim that moral emotions and moral cognition are *functionally* integrated in real-life moral situations, that is, that they operate in parallel and are mutually supporting to the more questionable idea that the two are *developmentally* integrated, that is, that they also develop in parallel. There are approaches to moral education such as Triune Ethics (see Narvaez, this volume) and Oser's framework of "learning from mistakes" (Oser & Spychiger, 2005), which are exemplary in their sensitivity to this critical distinction. But as this chapter has shown, some of the most widely adopted and popularly compelling approaches to social-emotional learning underestimate the extent to which support for the growth of an aspect of moral cognition such as social inferencing and that of the moral emotion empathy call for different educational responses.

References

Batson, C. D. (1991). *The altruism question: Toward a social-psychological answer.* Hillsdale, NJ: Erlbaum.

Bloom, P. (2004). *Descartes's baby: How the science of child development helps explain what makes us human.* New York: Basic Books.

Cahan, E. (2006). Toward a socially relevant science: Notes on the history of child development. In B. Beatty, E. D. Cahan, & J. Grant (Eds.), *When science encounters the child: Education, parenting and child welfare in 20th-century America* (pp. 16–43). New York: Teachers College Press.

Committee for Children. (2002). The importance of teaching social-emotional skills: Teacher's guide. Retrieved June 10, 2010, from http://www.cfchildren.org/media/files/Second%20Step%20Pre_K%20Review%20of%20Research.pdf

Crick, N. R., & Dodge, K. A. (1996). Social information-processing mechanisms in reactive and proactive aggression. *Child Development, 67*(3), 993–1002.

Davis, M. H. (1994). *Empathy: A social psychological approach.* Madison, WI: Brown & Benchmark.

D'Silva, K., Dugan, C., & McCarthy, L. (2004) Does treatment really make psychopaths worse? A review of the evidence. *Journal of Personality Disorders, 18*(2), 163–177.

Duffel, J. C., Beland, K., & Frey, K. (2006). The Second Step program: Social-emotional skills for violence prevention. In J. J. Elias & H. Arnold (Eds.), *The educator's guide to emotional intelligence and academic achievement: Emotional learning in the classroom* (pp. 161–171). Thousand Oaks, CA: Corwin Press.

Eisenberg, N., Murphy, B. C., & Shepard, S. (1997). The development of empathic accuracy. In W. Ickes (Ed.), *Empathic accuracy* (pp. 73–116). New York: Guilford Press.

Embry, D. D., Flannery, D. J., Vazsonyi, A. T., Powell, K. E., & Atha, H. (1996). PeaceBuilders: A theoretically driven, school-based model for early violence prevention. *American Journal of Preventive Medicine, 12*(5, Suppl.), 91–100.

Flannery, D. J., Liau, A. K., Powell, K. E., Vesterdal, W., Vazsonyi, A. T., Guo, S., et al. (2003). Initial behavior outcomes for the PeaceBuilders universal school-based violence prevention program. *Developmental Psychology, 30*(2), 292–308.

Flavell, J. H., Miller, P. H., & Miller, S. A. (2002). *Cognitive development* (4th ed.). Upper Saddle River, NJ: Prentice Hall.

Gibbs, J. (2003). *Moral development and reality: Beyond the theories of Kohlberg and Hoffman.* Thousand Oaks, CA: Sage.

Goleman, D. (1995). *Emotional intelligence.* New York: Bantam.

Gutzwiller-Helfenfinger, E., Gasser, L., & Malti, T. (2010). Moral emotions and moral judgments in children's narratives: Comparing real-life and hypothetical transgressions. In B. Latzko & T. Malti (Eds.), *Children's moral emotions and moral cognition: Developmental and educational perspectives. New Directions for Child and Adolescent Development, 129*, 11–31.

Hastings, P. D., Zahn-Waxler, C., Robinson, J., Usher, B., & Bridges, D. (2000). The development of concern for others in children with behavior problems. *Developmental Psychology, 36*, 531–546.

Higgins, E.T. (1981). Role taking and social judgment: Alternative developmental perspectives and processes. In J. H. Flavell & Lee Ross (Eds.), *Social cognitive development: Frontiers and possible futures* (pp. 119–153). Cambridge: Cambridge University Press.

Hoffman, M. L. (1981). Is altruism part of human nature? *Journal of Personality and Social Psychology*, 40(1), 121–137.

Hoffman, M. L. (2000). *Empathy and moral development: Implications for caring and justice.* Cambridge: Cambridge University Press.

Honig, M.-S., Leu, H. R., & Nissen, U. (1996). *Kinder und Kindheit: Soziokulturelle Muster—Sozialisationstheoretische Perspektiven.* [*Children and childhood: Sociocultural patterns—socialisation-theoretical perspectives*]. Weinheim, Munich: Juventa.

Izard, C., Fine, S., Schultz, D., Mostow, A., & Ackerman, B. (2001). Emotional knowledge and social behavior. *Psychological Science, 12*, 18–23.

Kohlberg, L. (1981). *Essays on moral development, Vol. 1: The philosophy of moral development. Moral stages and the idea of justice.* San Francisco: Harper & Row.

Kohlberg, L. (1984). *Essays on moral development, Vol. 2: The psychology of moral development. The Nature and validity of moral stages.* San Francisco: Harper & Row.

Kohut, H. (1959). Introspection, empathy and psychoanalysis. *Journal of the American Psychoanalytic Association, 7*, 459–483.

Krause, A., Şıkcan, S., & Wagner, P. (2004). *Kinderwelten: A national project for the dissemination and further development of the anti-bias approach in child care centers.* Berlin: Institute for the Situational Approach (ISTA).

Lapsley, D., & Hill, P. (2008). On dual processing and heuristic approaches to moral cognition. *Journal of Moral Education, 37*(3), 313–332.

Maxwell, B. (2008). *Professional ethics education: Studies in compassionate empathy.* Dordrecht: Springer.

Maxwell, B., & Reichenbach, R. (2007). Educating moral emotions: A praxiological analysis. *Studies in Philosophy and Education, 26*(2), 147–163.

Meyer, A. L., Farrell, A. D., Northup, W., Kung, E. M., & Plybon, L. (2001). *Promoting non-violence in middle schools: Responding in peaceful and positive ways (RIPP).* New York: Plenum.

Miller, P., Eisenberg, N., Fabes, R. A., & Shell, R. (1996). Relations of moral reasoning and vicarious emotion to young children's prosocial behavior towards peers and adults. *Developmental Psychology, 32*(2), 210–219.

Minnameier, G. (2010). The problem of moral motivation and the happy victimizer phenomenon: Killing two birds with one stone. In B. Latzko & T. Malti (Eds.), *Children's moral emotions and moral cognition: Developmental and educational perspectives. New Directions for Child and Adolescent Development, 129*, 55–75.

Nagel, T. (1970). *The possibility of altruism.* Oxford: Clarendon Press.

Narvaez, D. (2010). The emotional foundations of high moral intelligence. In B. Latzko & T. Malti (Eds.), Children's *moral emotions and moral cognition: Developmental and educational perspectives. New Directions for Child and Adolescent Development, 129*, 77–94.

Nussbaum, M. (1995). *Poetic justice.* Boston: Beacon Press.

Nussbaum, M. (2001). *Upheavals of thought: The intelligence of the emotions.* Cambridge: Cambridge University Press.

Oser, F., & Spychiger, M. (2005). *Lernen ist schmerzhaft. Zur Theorie des negativen Wissens und zur Praxis der Fehlerkultur.* [*Learning is painful. Towards a theory of negative knowledge and a practice of a culture of mistakes*]. Weinheim, Munich: Beltz.

Piaget, J. (1932). *The moral judgement of the child.* New York: Harcourt.

Rice, M. E., Harris, G. T., & Cormier, C. A. (1992). An evaluation of a maximum security therapeutic community for psychopaths and other mentally disordered offenders. *Law and Human Behavior, 16*(4), 399–412.

Seligman, M. E. P., & Csikszentmihalyi, M. (2000). Positive psychology: An introduction. *American Psychologist, 55*(1), 5–14.

Smith, A. (2009). *Theory of moral sentiments.* Norderstedt: GRIN Verlag. (Original work published 1759)

Tolan, P., & Guerra, N. (1994). *What works in reducing adolescent violence: An empirical review of the field.* Boulder, CO: The Center for the Study and Prevention of Violence.

Tulving, E. (1985). Memory and consciousness. *Canadian Psychology, 26*, 1–12.

Turiel, E. (1998). The development of morality. In W. Damon (Ed.), *Handbook of child psychology, Vol. 3: Social, emotional, and personality development* (pp. 863–932). New York: Wiley.

U.S. Department of Health and Human Services. (2001). *Youth violence: A report of the Surgeon General.* Rockville: U.S. Public Health Service, Office of the Surgeon General.

BRUCE MAXWELL is professor of education at the Université du Québec à Trois-Rivières and associated researcher at the University of Montreal Centre for Ethics Research. E-mail: bruce.maxwell@umontreal.ca, webpage: www.creum.umontreal.ca/spip.php?article 740.

SARAH DESROCHES is a doctoral student in integrated studies in education at McGill University. E-mail: sarahdesroches@gmail.com.

Minnameier, G. (2010). The problem of moral motivation and the happy victimizer phenomenon: Killing two birds with one stone. In B. Latzko & T. Malti (Eds.), *Children's moral emotions and moral cognition: Developmental and educational perspectives. New Directions for Child and Adolescent Development, 129*, 55–75. San Francisco: Jossey-Bass.

4

The Problem of Moral Motivation and the Happy Victimizer Phenomenon: Killing Two Birds with One Stone

Gerhard Minnameier

Abstract

One surprising feature of cognitive and emotional development in the moral domain is the so-called happy victimizer phenomenon, which is commonly explained by a lack of moral motivation. Concerning this general approach, there are two pieces of news in this chapter. The bad news is that moral motivation is a highly problematic concept and its purported theoretical role in moral functioning untenable. The good news is that the happy victimizer phenomenon can be explained without reference to something like "moral motivation." © *Wiley Periodicals, Inc.*

Introduction: Moral Motivation as a Solution and a Problem

The idea of a gap between moral reasoning and moral action has been long running in moral psychology and education and has led to a rather large body of literature with thorough theoretical analyses, empirical studies, and suggestions for bridging this purported gap (see e.g., Bebeau, 1994; Blasi, 1980, 1983, 1984; Kohlberg & Candee, 1984; Malti & Latzko, this volume; Nunner-Winkler, 1993; Oser, 1999; Rest, 1983, 1984; Rest, Narvaez, Bebeau, & Thoma, 1999; Thoma, 1994; see Bergman 2002 for an overview and detailed analysis). Most prominent in this respect is Rest's four component model, which consists of moral sensitivity, moral judgment, moral motivation, and moral character (see e.g., Rest et al., 1999, p. 101).

At issue here is the third component, "moral motivation." According to Rest it consists in selecting among competing values and deciding whether or not to fulfill one's moral ideal (1983, p. 564; 1984, pp. 27, 32). Thus, moral motivation is conceived as the driving force by which moral agents oblige themselves to follow the moral course of action instead of some other goal. And the relevance of moral motivation is exemplified by a study on children's reasoning and action in a situation concerning distributive justice (see Rest, 1984, p. 32). In this study, Damon (1977) asked young children how they think candy bars should be distributed as rewards for a task they had been given before. The children came up with different morally sensible dividing schemes. However, when they were given the candy bars and asked to actually give them out to their mates, they deviated from those schemes and allotted themselves a disproportionate number of candy bars.

This behavior is equivalent to the well-known prototypic stories on the happy victimizer phenomenon (see the review article by Arsenio, Gold, & Adams, 2006), and it is therefore almost natural that this phenomenon has been explained by a lack of moral motivation.

The happy victimizer phenomenon appears in middle childhood and has been described by various prominent researchers (Arsenio & Kramer, 1992; Lourenço, 1997; Keller et al., 2003; Malti & Latzko, this volume; Nunner-Winkler, 1999, 2007; Nunner-Winkler & Sodian, 1988). It consists in the fact that children who know moral rules (know that certain acts are immoral) nevertheless choose illicit alternatives to their own benefit. In particular, in the typical experimental setting, subjects attribute positive emotions to an actual victimizer (they are presented a picture story about stealing or other egoistic behavior and are asked how the victimizer feels). Arsenio et al., for instance, comment that "young children's empathic abilities, their understanding of moral rules, and their strong emotional ties to others make it seem implausible that they would simply expect victimizers to feel happy as a result of the gains produced by victimization. Yet, that is exactly what much of the research suggests" (2006, p. 585). There is a possibility, and the research on the phenomenon has revealed the validity of this point (see Keller, Lourenço, Malti, & Saalbach, 2003), that subjects might attribute positive emotions to the victimizer because they take her perspective and think she must feel good because she wanted to act in this way and got what she wanted. However, this does not explain the whole story, and in particular it does not explain the salience and dominance of personal interests in relation to the previously acquired understanding of moral rules that is typical of the five- to seven-year-olds' reasoning (see Arsenio et al., 2006, for an extensive discussion). Arsenio et al. come to the conclusion that "it would be a mistake to conclude that the happy victimizer expectancy is simply a methodological artifact" (2006, p. 595).

On the standard interpretation, this phenomenon is explained by a lack of moral motivation. Subjects are said to possess moral knowledge, but not the complementary motivational powers to suppress or subordinate their present inclinations. What's more, some—like Rest, but contrary to Kohlberg and Candee (1984)—believe that moral motivation develops independently from moral judgment. Nunner-Winkler even holds that the development of moral motivation is much harder and much more important than that of moral judgment: "Moral development is a two-layered process: The first step is the early and universal acquisition of moral knowledge, the second is the slow and hard process of building up moral motivation" (1993, p. 281; see also 2007, p. 412).

However, moral motivation is a tricky concept and far more problematic than the literature on the four-component model and the happy victimizer tells us. In particular, there has been a long and deep philosophical debate on this issue that has just been ignored by psychologists, although the philosophical and Rest's psychological concept of moral motivation are equivalent. In light of these philosophical analyses, however, moral motivation might have to be rejected—at least this is the conclusion of the present chapter. And thus, the happy victimizer would need a new foundation, which is also delivered in this chapter.

This philosophical debate will be reviewed in the next section, so as to reveal the problematic status of "moral motivation." In this debate, the proponents claim that moral motivation is needed to bridge moral judgment to moral action, whereas the opponents hold that moral judgments are self-motivating and reject the entire notion of moral motivation. The former position is called "moral externalism" (because motivation is seen as external to moral judgment), the latter "moral internalism."

The controversy was triggered off by the observation that people can actually act deliberately against their own moral convictions without any feeling of remorse (e.g. Foot, 1972), which squares with the concept of the happy victimizer. The philosophical problem as such, however, can be traced back at least to the era of Enlightenment (see Darwell,

1995). In the following sections we shall first explore this controversy about moral internalism and externalism, where a weak form of internalism will be supported. Based on this position, the notion of moral motivation will be rejected as theoretically void and practically superfluous. This immediately raises the question of how one could explain the happy victimizer phenomenon. In the subsequent sections this problem will be solved by accommodating the happy victimizer as a special type of moral *reasoning*, which is explicated in a neo-Kohlbergian framework of stages.

Moral Internalism versus Moral Externalism: On the Sources of Motivational Powers and the Concept of Moral Motivation

As already mentioned above, the problem of moral motivation is well known in moral philosophy and has been discussed very deeply in this camp. Therefore let us exploit this rich source of established knowledge. Some philosophers hold that moral motivation is necessary for (the explanation of) moral agency; others deny that. The two opposed positions are called "moral internalism" and "moral externalism."

Moral internalism expresses the simple but straightforward view that moral judgments are intrinsically motivating in that thinking something to be the right thing to do implies the motivation to bring this about and to act accordingly. Indeed, moral internalism rests on the conviction that it would be practically irrational for a subject S to hold that A would be the proper course of action and still decide not to do A (Smith 1994/2005, p. 61).

However, moral internalism is challenged by the common experience that people fairly often fail to do what they themselves deem right. Hence, so the argument goes, internalism must be false and there must be a separate process taking place to establish the commitment to do A above and beyond the belief that A ought to be done (e.g., Brink, 1989, pp. 42–45, 1997; Foot, 1972; Railton, 1986). This is the externalist position that assumes a logical and factual independence of moral motivation and moral judgment.

Historically, and perhaps surprisingly, a key figure having established this latter view is Kant (see Ameriks, 2006; Homann, 2004). He realized that the categorical imperative is a (transcendental) fact of reason that people may see but still fail to incorporate in their actions. The will, or volition, is conceived of as the instance by which insight becomes implemented in empirical action. The first section of his *Groundwork of the Metaphysics of Morals* begins with the words, "Nothing can possibly be conceived in the world, or even out of it, which can be called good, without qualification, except a good will" (4.393). If it were not for this free will, the moral person would be fully determined by her insights, which violates the principle of free choice. Therefore, the moral "must," in Kant's sense, cannot possibly be a causal "must" (Ameriks, 2006, p. 15).

However, in the Kantian framework this problem of freedom results directly from the supposed transcendental nature of the categorical imperative. If the moral principle is not conceived as transcendental and thus relegated entirely to the individual's personal reflection, her moral judgment will always be a product of the free will in terms of autonomous decision making.

Apart from this purely Kantian predicament, there is also the universal problem of determining the proper source of the purported moral motivation. Supposing that moral motivation does not result directly from moral judgment, how could it be explained? Why ought a moral subject to be moral and domesticate her inclinations, if not for the very fact this is what morality itself requires? In other words: How can moral motivation be explained from an externalist point of view? So far, moral motivation appears as only an ad hoc construction to explain why people may fail to live up to their own moral standards. The invoked moral motivation itself, however, still remains to be explained.

Of course, people may always be irrational, weak, or careless and might regret their moral shortcomings later on. But this is not the issue. Rather, externalists claim that immorality may be fully rational and that therefore moral motivation is analytically separate from moral judgment (see, e.g., Brink, 1997, pp. 18–21). And where immorality is held to be rational, there is no reason for having a bad conscience. Their claim squares with Rest's third component (see above).

Consider Rest's and Damon's candy bar example. The agents deliberately go back on their own moral principles and feel no remorse when allotting themselves a disproportionate number of candy bars as reward. If they felt bad about that, they would have to be regarded as morally motivated, that is, they would feel committed to a fair scheme of distributing the candy bars, in principle, which they would have violated for some non-moral reason. In this case, their failure to act according to their moral voice would have to be put down to a lack of ego strength or weakness of will, which belongs to the fourth component ("moral character"), not the third. It has to be clear that we are not arguing about the question of moral character (or as I would prefer to say, "moral volition"), but only about the logically prior question, whether one thinks one should follow the moral course of action or not.

Internalism, in its weak form, does not deny that people may go back on their moral principles, but only that this is done on pain of "practical irrationality" (provided the moral judgment was valid and thus not irrational in itself). Hence, Smith, for example, supports the following version of internalism: "If an agent judges that it is right for her to φ in circumstances C, then either she is motivated to φ in C or she is practically irrational" (1994, p. 61). And he clarifies that "agents who judge it right to act in various ways are so motivated, and necessarily so, absent the distorting influences of weakness of the will and other similar forms of practical unreason on their motivations" (Smith, 1994, p. 61; see also, Smith, 2008). There has been some puzzlement about Smith's notion of rationality or having reason to φ in C (see, e.g., Sayre-McCord, 1997). Much of the argument is about the question of justification, which, however, is perhaps unnecessary (see also Smith, 1997, especially pp. 101–106). Apart from the problems of epistemological internalism and externalism, the only important point is whether the subject believes she ought to φ in C, or whether she is uncertain about this question. At least, this would explain why the moral puzzles invoked by Haidt (2001) are unproblematic with respect to Smith's analysis. These stories are all about acts that contradict common morality (like incest, for example), but where all possible harm is excluded, so that the question really arises, what the agents should do. Usually, subjects tend to reject the generally "immoral" actions (following their gut feelings), although they fail to have conclusive reasons why this should be so. It might be argued that these subjects think that (in the example and in this case) an act of incestuous behavior might be acceptable or even morally right, and still have a desire (their gut feelings) contrary to their reasons. However, this would be a distortion of the notion of *belief*, for they are still uncertain in this case and therefore not in a position to have a (sufficiently strong) belief, or else we could say that they believe what their guts tell them, which entails that it is entirely rational for them not to indulge in the incestuous act.

Note that this version of internalism not only allows for distorting influences, but also relativizes moral obligation to circumstances C and to the agent's believing in her obligation. Hence the possibility that the agent knows what is generally right to do, but does not accept the respective maxim either in general or in her particular situation, is clearly ruled out. And to my mind this is correct if the agent is to be ascribed a moral judgment that she ought to φ in C.

The conclusion to be drawn so far is that if we were to accept moral externalism, we would have to answer at least two questions:

1. How could moral motivation be explained apart from the agent's belief that she ought to φ in C?
2. How could anybody reasonably believe that she ought to φ in C and remain indifferent, owing to a lack of moral motivation and absent distortions such as weakness of will (which belong to the fourth component)?

The following section tries to show that there are no convincing answers to either of these questions. Those readers who already believe that moral externalism is false could skip this section and proceed to the next.

The Problem of Explaining Moral Motivation

As to the first question there appear to be no valid explanations (see Smith 1994/2005; pp. 71–76; Homann, 2004, pp. 37–48). Ever since Hume, reference has been made to inborn faculties, cultural influences, and the like (see Homann, 2004, pp. 34–36; Smith, 1994/2005, pp. 92–129). However, this does not explain much, if it explains anything at all because it only shifts the explanatory burden. One would have to explain not only why and how, for example, inborn faculties have evolved, but also and especially how they actualized. This would be the question of how moral motivation is brought about, or in other words, *how motivation is motivated.* Therefore, this line of reasoning only (mis)leads into an infinite regress.

Furthermore, in moral psychology moral motivation is typically explained with reference to the moral self (or moral identity) that is thought to develop independently of moral understanding (see Blasi, 1984, 1995; Damon, 1984). However, as Sokol (2007) points out, this separation involves a concept of the self as a kind of homunculus above and beyond—here—moral cognition, a ghost in the machine that steers and interferes. At any rate, the conceptual separation entails the need to explain precisely how the two systems are supposed to evolve and to interact. This is an open question for advocates of moral motivation.

Finally, moral motivation is reduced to a kind of habit, if not to an obsession, just because it is divorced from moral judgment. What should drive an agent to φ in C, if not her conviction that she ought to φ in C? Besides, this raises the question whether moral motivation in this sense could be a suitable aim of education, especially in light of the fact that morally motivated people would be inclined to act to their personal detriment. Might the call for moral motivation not express a rather rigid view of morality, one in which people are expected to harm themselves for the sake of some moral ideal? And if so, how far should that go and could that be justifiable? (For an answer to this question see the following section.)

Concerning this last question, Brink (1989, 1997; following Foot, 1972) argues that the idea of a principled amoralist is possible and coherent—where "principled" means that amoralism is not due to psychological interference in the sense of distortions mentioned above, but rests on "conceptions of morality and practical reason according to which moral requirements need not have rational authority" (1997, p. 18). For the moral internalist, however, "it must be conceptually impossible for someone to recognize a moral consideration or assert a moral judgment and remain unmoved" (Brink, 1989, p. 46). The purported coherence of the principled amoralist is derived as described below.

As long as we associate morality with an impartial point of view that imposes other-regarding duties and accept an agent-centered conception of practical reason that rests on instrumental or prudential conceptions of practical reason, it seems we must recognize the possibility of moral requirements that it is not irrational to disobey.

1. Moral requirements include impartial other-regarding obligations that do not apply to agents in virtue of their aims or interests.
2. Rational action is action that achieves the agent's aims or promotes her interests.
3. There are circumstances in which fulfilling other-regarding obligations would not advance the agent's aims or interests.
4. Hence, there can be (other-regarding) moral requirements such that failure to act on them is not irrational. (Brink, 1997, pp. 18–19)

The force of the argument hinges entirely on the plausibility of separating morality on the one hand and practical reason on the other. However, this distinction seems to beg the question, because, first, there is no reason to restrict the concept of practical reason to the agent-centered (egocentric) perspective as Brink does in (1) and (2). In fact, morality always tries to mediate between different agents' inclinations or claims and thus aims at and results in a second-order practical reasoning or second-order desire. If it were not for this second-order desire, no one would engage in moral reasoning in the first place. I believe that much confusion in the debate has arisen from an unclear notion of desire in the context of moral motivation (see also Ameriks, 2006, pp. 6–7) and also of moral belief (which, to my mind, cannot plausibly be deprived of the desire to act according to it, as, for example, Zangwill [2003], assumes). In Zangwill's case, a moral belief is taken as a part of common moral knowledge about rules and precincts. So, for example, we know that we should be polite, grateful, considerate, or whatever. Such moral knowledge, of course, does not oblige us to act accordingly; hence, it does not necessarily motivate us. However, such moral knowledge is not be confused with moral judgment, which would have to deal with exactly this question of whether common moral precincts should be binding for me in circumstances C.

Second, the very question, raised in (3), of whether one ought to fulfill one's aims or interests (first-order desires) or one's moral obligations (second-order desires) might—and, to my mind, must—be understood as *a moral question in itself* and thus requiring a moral rather than a merely prudential answer (see also the following section). Hence, (4) might somehow be true, but the rationality of acting against certain moral requirements could then only be established on further and overriding moral grounds. If so, the problem is not that moral judgments would not result in moral motivation but that moral judgments sometimes have to be revised or seem inappropriate as such. Consequently, Brink's, and Foot's, amoralist could turn out to be no more than a puzzled or wavering moralist. The different ways in which the "amoralist" might be reconstructed as a "moralist" are spelled out in the following sections.

A Solution to the Problem of Moral Motivation

The internalism we ought to discuss and which I would like to defend is labeled "appraiser internalism" by Brink (see 1989, pp. 45–47; 1997, p. 18). Appraiser internalism holds that moral motivation depends on the appraisal of a certain moral judgment. To motivate, moral obligations must not only be known (as established rules in a certain community or context) but are to be endorsed by the moral subject. Now let us recall the four components of morality set forth by Rest (1984, p. 27; see above):

I. To interpret the situation in terms of how one's actions affect the welfare of others.
II. To formulate what a moral course of action would be; to identify the moral ideal in a specific situation.
III. To select among competing value outcomes of ideals, the one to act on; deciding whether or not to try to fulfill one's moral ideal.
IV. To execute and implement what one intends to do.

As already mentioned, these components are labeled *moral sensitivity (I)*, *moral judgment (II)*, *moral motivation (III)*, and *moral character (IV)* (Rest et al., 1999, p. 101). It should be noted, first, that without moral sensitivity there would be no moral problem and hence no further moral reflection or processing. Turned the other way round, the very fact that someone makes a moral decision implies that she is sensitive to the respective moral problem and has a *desire* to work out what she (or anybody else) ought to do in that situation. Rest claims that the relationship between the four components is not linear, so that the components could interact in different ways (see, e.g., 1984, p. 33–36; Narvaez & Rest, 1995, p. 397–398). However, these relations and processes have not been revealed and analyzed systematically, nor does a non-linear model make sense, as long as the model rests on an action-theoretic background, which clearly is the case. Moreover, the definitions of the components are such that each component builds on its successor(s). That there are feedback loops, so that, for example, prior judgments and practical experience have a bearing on subsequent moral sensitivity, is granted. However, this would not violate the linearity-assumption and therefore be no point against the supposed linearity of the psychological process of moral functioning in a given situation. Consequently, a moral belief in the form of a moral judgment cannot be conceived as an act of "cold cognition," rather is it already motivated by the insight in the given moral problem and—*having* that problem—a desire to solve it.

Second, moral judgment tells us what to do in that specific situation (not just in general). Hence, Rest's view, as well as Kohlberg's, converges with appraiser internalism in this respect. Furthermore, situational adaptations are excluded from the possible obstacles between moral judgment and the motivational impetus because the peculiarities of the situation are dealt with in the course of moral judgment.

Excluded are, third, psychological distortions like weakness of will, because this is to be subsumed under the fourth component. This also matches with our discussion above because such influences were not treated as problems of moral motivation (at least with respect to the weaker form of moral internalism which is the one at issue in the present context; see also Brink, 1997, pp. 7, 16–17). Brink, as an externalist, explicitly concedes that it is possible to endorse a necessary connection between judgment and motivation "without supposing there is a necessary connection between motivation and action" (1997, p. 17; see also above). The former relates to the move from II to III, whereas the latter relates to the move from III to IV.

Given this analysis one may wonder how one ought to carry out the selection described as Component III. What grounds, apart from the ones already mentioned and included in the other three components, could be imagined that take us to a decision whether or not we ought to try to fulfill our moral duties? I cannot think of any. That is, I could think of only two kinds of grounds which, however, clearly belong to other components. It may be, and certainly is often the case, that someone acts in ways that she herself cannot approve of. Greed, jealousy, or weakness of will may cause us to go back on our own principles. Such cases, however, typically create a bad conscience and therefore relate to the fourth component (in terms of a failure to actualize one's proper intentions). Sometimes a bad conscience might be avoided by inventing ad hoc explanations of why it was right to act as one did, which then relates to specific situational aspects (that lead to a revision of the original moral judgment). This brings us to the second type of grounds, those which do not result in a bad conscience. If so, one has to have reasons that justify the act, and this means to have *moral* reasons. Such grounds, therefore, belong to the second component, not to the mysterious third one. In opposition to my solution, one might consider Brink's argument in favor of the amoralist (discussed above). However, I take it that the gist of his point dissolves in the light of my argumentation against moral motivation in the preceding section. He holds that (other-regarding) moral obligations may conflict with the agent's interests to the effect that the agent might choose the non-moral alternative without being practically irrational. On my account, the question of what to do in this situation is a downright moral one and therefore fully covered by the process of moral reflection and judgment. Yet one problem remains. What about situations in which the agent is unsure and has doubts whether she ought to act on a particular norm (see Brink, 1997, p. 19). In this case one might say that moral obligations lack authority for the agent, and thus it would not be irrational not to comply with them.

To cut a long story short, my solution to the problem of moral motivation is to conclude that moral motivation in the sense of Component III is theoretically empty and practically superfluous. Any question as to whether one ought to meet a certain moral requirement or not is in itself a moral question and must lead to moral reflection, unless the matter is left open (this also applies to Brink's opposition of other-regarding obligations and the agent's interests in his defense of the amoralist [see the last section], which I consider defeated by the present argument). Once one has made up one's mind, eventually, one has to act according to it on pain of practical irrationality and self-reproach. This, at least, is the thesis.

It may, of course, well be the case that this reasoning is split into the process of forming an idea (an initial judgment) and the subsequent consideration of pros and cons that might lead either to the acceptance or rejection of a certain principle in a given situation. Such inferential processes can even be tracked down fairly well, e.g., with the Peircean triad of abduction, deduction, and induction (see, e.g., Minnameier, 2004). However, that does not change the fact that this all belongs to one overall process of moral judgment rather than anything beyond it.

Furthermore, on the assumption that the happy victimizer phenomenon refers to a kind of defect owing to underdeveloped moral motivation or a lack of integration of moral cognition and the (im)moral self, one may be astounded at the fact that happy victimizers are by no means the exception, but rather appear to be the rule among five- to seven-year-olds. Hence, if it is more or less normal for children of a certain age to pass through a phase in which they might be prone to "happy victimizer" reasons and emotion attributions, an alternative way of dealing with the problem would be to try to reconstruct the "happy victimizing" as a special form of moral reasoning and understanding.

A Neo-Kohlbergian Stage Theory: Accommodating the Happy Victimizer on a Particular Stage of Moral Reasoning

As mentioned above, the happy victimizer phenomenon constitutes an especially strong point against moral internalism because in such cases agents not only fail to act according to their moral convictions but on top of that seem to be most sanguine about that, far from having a bad conscience. This seems to be the true puzzle.

However, if it is true that people do *judge* it right for them not to do A, even though they know that A is right in general or by common standards, it may be asked whether such a deliberate judgment against received moral precepts were not to be reconstructed as a downright *moral* one.

It has already been pointed out that in general moral, reasoning certain moral courses of action might be rejected due to situational hindrances (e.g., where moral behavior of one competitor in the market might be exploited by others). The happy victimizer, however, requires a different explanation. Happy-victimizer-like moral functioning appears—and vanishes—in a typical age range. Because at that age, happy victimizers are the rule rather than the exception, the happy victimizer phenomenon seems to denote a distinct developmental phase that normal children have to go through.

Strange as this move may perhaps appear at first glance, a similar attempt has been made by Kohlberg when he realized that adolescents apparently regressed from Stage 4 to Stage 2 (see Kohlberg, & Kramer, 1969) and subsequently reconstructed their moral points of view in terms of a transitional Stage 4 ½ (Kohlberg & Candee, 1984) or Stage 4/5 (Colby & Kohlberg, 1987, p. 101). So, there seem to be good reasons to deal with the happy victimizer in terms of a *stage of moral reasoning*, especially because it was also argued that Stage 4/5 is really no transitional stage but one of its own (see also Minnameier, 2009).

In the following, we will explore this possibility in connection with an enhanced neo-Kohlbergian stage taxonomy, in which the happy victimizer can be neatly accommodated, and then underpin this reconstruction with reference to Kohlberg's—and Piaget's—own conceptualizations. This taxonomy and its underlying developmental principles are laid out in detail in Minnameier (2000 and 2001; see also 2005; 2009; 2010), so a brief sketch may—and will have to—do in the present context.

A Neo-Kohlbergian Stage Taxonomy

The main constructive principles for the proposed architecture of moral cognition are derived from Piaget and Garcia (1989), who assume a dialectical sequence of stages and levels throughout development as a whole (note that Piaget has also reconceived his stages of intellectual development accordingly). Thus, development is thought to proceed in a succession of stage-triads, each of which consists of three characteristic types, which Piaget and Garcia call "intra," "inter," and "trans" (see Figure 4.1). These forms could also be paraphrased as differentiation (intra), reciprocal relation (inter), and integration (trans) (see Piaget & Garcia, 1989, pp. 273–274). Piaget and Garcia speak of "transformation" because objects can be transformed into each other. What is crucial here is a common denominator, which enables such a transformation. I prefer the term (reciprocal) "relation" because especially in the context of moral thinking, individual perspectives are not literally transformed into each other, but only balanced in a certain way.

This is to say that a given object of cognition is first differentiated into various instances of a "form." In the moral domain one is able to differentiate perspectives systematically. Whereas from an egocentric point of view one assumes that others think like oneself and fails to make the distinction, one can now address the other's point of view independently. However, at such an initial *intra-stage* it is yet impossible to put these

Figure 4.1. Stage Types and Justice Operations

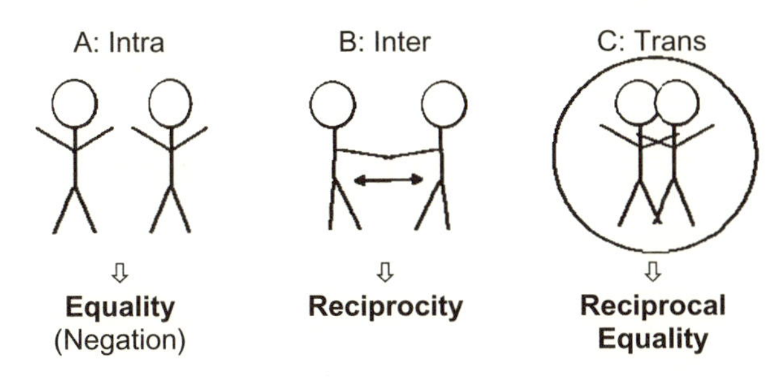

perspectives into relation. One can only take one at a time, see that they are different, and accept them each for what they are. Therefore, this type of reasoning is said to incorporate the justice operation of equality (all perspectives being regarded as equally valid), but not that of reciprocity. Note, in this respect, that the basic moral operation is not to *mediate between* different perspectives but—logically prior—simply to *distinguish and recognize* them *as such and as equally valid as one's own* (see Mackie, 1977).

At the "inter"-stage the previously differentiated perspectives are *reciprocally* related to each other by a mechanism that mediates *between* them, but in a way that disregards the individuality of those perspectives and the differences between them (as, for instance, in the "tit for tat" principle). The latter is only achieved at the "trans"-stage, where the inter-individual differences are taken into account, which results in a reintegration of the differentiated individual perspectives into a new and complex whole, yielding what I call "reciprocal equality." It is crucial, however, that such a complex whole can in turn be differentiated into a (new) variety of forms, which then constitutes a higher-order "intra-stage." And so development is supposed to continue in a hierarchy of embedded stage-triads (see Figure 4.2).

According to Piaget and Garcia (1989, p. 173), each triad of "stages" is thought to be embedded in "levels." In the present framework, we differentiate three layers, so that there are three "substages" in a stage and three stages in each of three levels. For more details on this cognitive architecture see Minnameier (2000, 2001, 2005, 2009). Two clarifications may, however, be in order here.

First, "levels" in the present framework do not reflect Kohlberg's trichotomy of preconventional, conventional, and postconventional reasoning (see also Gibbs, 2003, p. 61–69 for a critique of this classification), but constitute the three areas of morality, ethics, and meta-ethics. Morality concerns first-order rules and principles of right behavior. Ethics treats questions of how to set up such rules in society and to what extent or under what conditions individuals are obliged to follow established rules and

Figure 4.2. Illustration of the Stage Hierarchy's Formal Structure and the Place of the Happy Victimizer

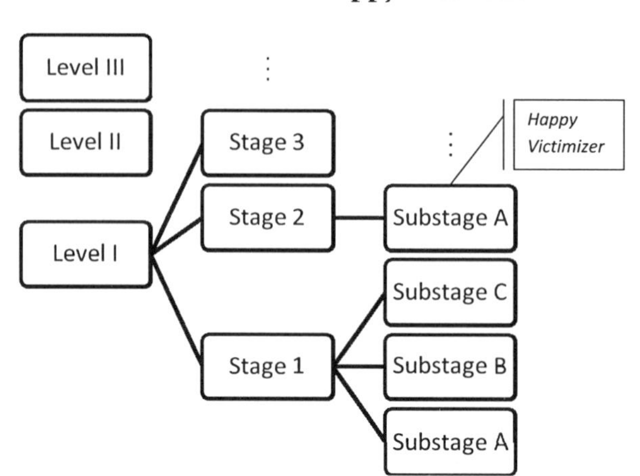

laws. Meta-ethics relates to the foundations of ethics, that is, the question why humans should be moral at a ll (from a rational point of view) and how they can be moral, provided that neither moral nor ethical principles can be discovered empirically or derived from nature (as Greek, Roman, and scholastic philosophers have always thought they could). This new reconstruction of levels also endorses Eckensberger's critique of Kohlberg in which he claimed that a major breach is between Kohlberg Stages 3 and 4, rather than between 2 and 3 or 4 and 5, respectively (cf. Eckensberger & Reinshagen 1980, pp. 100–105; see also Eckensberger, 2006).

Second, Kohlberg's substages (or types) reflect, to some extent, the differentiation on the smallest scale of the new taxonomy, although they do not fall into the same stage categories. For instance, Kohlberg Stage 3A is equivalent to his original "good boy–nice girl" interpretation of Stage 3, whereas Stage 3B stands for basic universalized interpersonal ideals (see Gibbs, 2003, p. 67). The "good boy–nice girl" concept (in the sense of being considerate would relate to I2C (i.e., Level I, Stage 2, Substage C) in the alternative taxonomy, whereas universalized interpersonal ideals is equivalent to II1a (i.e., Level II, Stage 1, Substage A). So there may be a great difference, even in terms of entire "stages," between two adjacent Kohlbergian substages/types.

The Happy Victimizer Reconstructed

As for the happy victimizer, we needn't explain the whole taxonomy, but only remain in the context in which this form of moral reasoning is localized, and this is at the lower end of the taxonomy (see Figure 4.2). To understand how it comes about in the course of moral development, let us start at the presumed beginning of moral reasoning and explain the developmental steps from Stage I1A to Stage I2A.

Moral thinking, even in its very basic form, requires that one is able to put oneself into the shoes of others because otherwise there would be no moral problem (at best one of prudence). Therefore, moral thinking has to start with an intra-stage at which one realizes that others have feelings and wishes just like oneself, so that empathic role taking in its most simple form is possible for the individual (Stage I1A). This is when children understand that they hurt someone, that others also want to play, eat, be loved, caressed, and so on.

The next step is to reciprocally relate these perspectives by implementing reciprocal exchange schemes such as taking turns, sharing and dividing equally (Stage I1b), which, however, is only just if both sides are in similar positions. If, on the other hand, someone is, say, better off than the other, then an equal share would possibly not be a fair share. Therefore, the simple reciprocity rule would have to be enhanced by addressing the initial differences to attain a just solution in the end. Following this line of reasoning, (that is, Stage I1c) the not-so-well-off person would have to be allotted more than the well-off. A typical example is that children donate some of their money for poor children in the world, without expecting anything in return. We know from a large body of research that even small children before and at kindergarten age are capable of such kinds of moral reasoning and perspective taking (see e.g., Hannaford, 1985; Kochanska, 1993; Turiel, 1998).

Now the crucial point with respect to the happy victimizer phenomenon is that throughout these first three stages children accept moral rules out of empathy and insight into others' needs and desires. They feel with other people and are *willing* to help them or comply with them. So it is assumed that whenever they see someone in need and know they *could* help, then they would also *want* to help (unless their own needs were superior), not that they *oblige* themselves against their personal inclinations. Recent research has revealed very clearly that sympathy and prosocial behavior are highly correlated, even among children with apparently low "moral motivation" (see Malti, Gummerum, Keller, & Buchmann, 2009).

However, children will come to experience that different interests may not mesh with each other. In particular, they will also learn that they might be used by others, that others may force them to do things they do not like, and perhaps in the name of morality (e.g., "You will do your best friend a favor, won't you?"). Moreover, some simply will not be willing to share with or to care for them. These behaviors may be thought of as morally wrong, but the question is how to (re)act to them from a moral point of view and what moral principle could serve as a guideline.

Thus, although being nice and considerate may still be regarded as the moral course of action, in general, one also recognizes that *everybody has interests to pursue* and that these may well conflict with each other. At the same time, the authority of moral rules, and thus moral heteronomy (in Piaget's sense), is diminished. Hence, the moral subject might argue that sometimes you have to take your share, or that you *don't have to do* what you *don't want to do*. Given that everybody pursues their own interests, why should you care for others, if you have no intrinsic desire to do so? One recognizes that the situation is the same for everybody—which makes for the equality relation according to Stage I2A (see Figure 4.1)—but because one is in one's own shoes, one pursues one's own interests. There is a risk of being revenged or punished, of course, but this simply has to be taken into account.

Later on, these competing interests are inter-individually regulated by mutual promises and deals, where the agreement establishes the reciprocal relation (because the interests can as yet not be balanced from a neutral or overarching point of view). This is Stage I2B. At I2C one is able to take such a superior perspective and is able to weigh individual interests independently and disinterestedly. At Stage I2C one may therefore yield to someone's interests when it is clear that these are more important than one's own. For instance, one lets people in a hurry skip a queue, or the druggist—in the Heinz dilemma—lets Heinz have the drug because Heinz needs it desperately and the druggist will not suffer from giving the drug away. Again, this is thought to be equivalent to the "good boy—good girl" type of reasoning in Kohlberg's sense.

The Happy Victimizer and Kohlberg's Stage 2

This sequence from I2A to I2C can be found in Piaget's (1932/1977) data, where he refers to "equity" (e.g., pp. 275, 305–306) when he means what I have called "reciprocal equality," which is the operation typical of all C-substages. And Piaget also outlines that children show capricious changes between egoism and sympathy when they move beyond heteronomous morality (pp. 306–307). This may also be indicative of the emphasis that is laid on personal interests at Stage I2A and thus of a happy victimizer kind of moral thinking.

Furthermore, if a child or anyone reasons in such a way (i.e., according to I2A), this first of all seems to be largely equivalent with Kohlberg's Stage 2. After all, a person at Kohlberg Stage 2 is said to follow rules only when it is to her immediate interest and that she acts to meet her own interests and needs and lets others do the same (1984, p. 174; Colby & Kohlberg, 1987, p. 19). Basically, "(t)here is an awareness that each person has interests to pursue and that these may conflict" (Colby & Kohlberg, 1987, p. 26). This is exactly what is claimed for Stage I2A, and the only problem from the point of view of Kohlberg's stages is that he conflates this type of moral reasoning with others (at least with I2B) and thus blurs his own notion of Stage 2.

As far as this argument is valid (and the research on the cognitive aspects of happy victimizing would support this interpretation; see Arsenio et al., 2006, pp. 587, 592), then the happy victimizer phenomenon might also be explained in terms of Kohlberg Stage 2 moral reasoning. And if this is true, there is no need to invoke a lack of moral motivation to explain the phenomenon, even from a classical Kohlbergian point of view.

According to our structural developmental approach, children's moral and emotional abilities that Arsenio et al. claim to be established by the age of five years are covered by the development across Stages I1A to I1C. And it is evident that children even before kindergarten age possess at least part of them. Conversely, there is "robust evidence that it is not typically before the ages of six or seven that children begin to associate moral emotions, such as sadness, guilt, or remorse, with immoral conduct" (Krettenauer, Malti, & Sokol, 2008, p. 223, see also Lagattuta, 2005). This seeming inconsistence vanishes in the light of our analysis because those moral emotions are linked with a sense of moral obligation that children can only grasp when they understand and accept moral duties above and beyond their sympathy with others, a concept of morality that integrates the very fact that different individuals pursue competing and mutually incompatible interests.

Thus, the happy victimizer cannot only be accommodated as a form of moral reasoning in the proposed neo-Kohlbergian framework, but just as well, at least in principle, in Kohlberg's own taxonomy. Consequently, there is no need to employ moral motivation to explain the phenomenon.

Conclusion

Moral motivation has turned out to be a highly problematic concept, both from the point of view of moral psychology and moral philosophy, and flawed in the light of our analysis in this chapter. As an alternative approach, a weak kind of "moral internalism" has been presented and defended. According to this position, moral motivation in the sense in which the term is also used in moral psychology is entailed by moral reasoning and as such already implicit in the very engagement in moral reasoning. This is not to be confused, however, with the subsequent volitional process of putting one's thoughts into action, which may be labeled ego strength, or moral character, and which is identical with Rest's "Component 4." As far as "moral motivation" is thought to relate to either this component or the first component of moral sensitivity, there is no problem with it (at least none is claimed in the present chapter). This might have to be (re)considered by those who still support the concept (cf., e.g., Bergman, 2002, for an overview and discussion of the different points of view).

As a consequence, the happy victimizer phenomenon has to be explained in a different way, and in the light of moral internalism a cognitivist approach would be the natural kind of answer to this question. We showed that a neo-Kohlbergian theory does the job and allows us to reconstruct the development of "happy victimizers" as well as how this particular moral point of view is overcome (and yes, it is a certain moral point of view, not an immoral one—or at best to be considered as immoral with respect to the higher stages). Besides, even if one is not willing to endorse the suggested theory, it would still be possible to interpret the "happy victimizer" in terms of Kohlberg's Stage 2 and the preceding types of moral reasoning in terms of his Stage 1. Hence, there is no need for the awkward and theoretically cumbersome notion of a *separate* process of moral motivation.

References

Ameriks, K. (2006). Kant and motivational externalism. In H. F. Klemme, M Kühn, & D. Schönecker (Eds.), *Moralische Motivation: Kant und die Alternativen* [Moral motivation: Kant and the alternatives] (pp. 3–22). Hamburg: Meiner.

Arsenio, W. F., Gold, J., & Adams, E. (2006). Children's conceptions and displays of moral emotions. In M. Killen & J. G. Smetana (Eds.), *Handbook of moral development* (pp. 581–609). Mahwah, NJ: Erlbaum.

Arsenio, W. F., & Kramer, R. (1992). Victimizers and their victims: Children's conceptions of the mixed emotional consequences of victimization. *Child Development, 63*, 915–927.

Bebeau, M. J. (1994). Influencing the moral dimensions of dental practice. In J. R. Rest & D. Narváez (Eds.), *Moral development in the professions: Psychology and applied ethics* (pp. 121–146). Hillsdale, NJ: Erlbaum.

Bergman, R. (2002). Why be moral? A conceptual model from developmental psychology. *Human Development, 45*, 104–124.

Blasi, A. (1980). Bridging moral cognition and moral action: A critical review of the literature. *Psychological Bulletin, 88*, 1–45.

Blasi, A. (1983). Moral cognition and moral action: A theoretical perspective. *Developmental Review, 3*, 178–210.

Blasi, A. (1984). Moral identity: Its role in moral functioning. In W. M. Kurtinez & J. L. Gewirtz (Eds.), *Morality, moral behavior, and moral development* (pp. 128–139). New York: Wiley.

Blasi, A. (1995). Moral understanding and the moral personality: The process of moral integration. In W. M. Kurtinez & J. L. Gewirtz (Eds.), *Moral development: An introduction* (pp. 229–253). Boston: Allyn and Bacon.

Brink, D. O. (1989). *Moral realism and the foundations of ethics*. Cambridge, UK: Cambridge University Press.

Brink, D. O. (1997). Moral motivation. *Ethics, 108*, 4–32.

Colby, A., & Kohlberg, L. (1987). *The measurement of moral judgment: Vol. I. Theoretical foundations and research validation*. Cambridge, UK: Cambridge University Press.

Damon, W. (1977). *The social world of the child*. San Francisco: Jossey-Bass.

Damon, W. (1984). Self-understanding and moral development from childhood to adolescence. In W. M. Kurtines & J. L. Gewirtz (Eds.), *Morality, moral behavior, and moral development* (pp. 109–127). New York: Wiley.

Darwell, S. (1995). *The British moralists and the internal 'ought': 1640–1740*. Cambridge, UK: Cambridge University Press.

Eckensberger, L. H. (2006). Contextualizing moral judgment: Challenges of interrelating the normative (ought judgments) and the descriptive (knowledge of facts), the cognitive and the affective. In L. Smith & J. Vonèche (Eds.), *Norms in human development* (pp. 141–168). Cambridge, UK: Cambridge University Press.

Eckensberger, L. H., & Reinshagen, H. (1980). Kohlbergs Stufentheorie der Entwicklung des Moralischen Urteils: Ein Versuch ihrer Reinterpretation im Bezugsrahmen handlungstheoretischer Konzepte[Kohlberg's stage theory of the development of moral judgment: An attempt at reinterpretation in the context of action theoretical concepts]. In L. H. Eckensberger & R. K. Silbereisen (Eds.), *Entwicklung sozialer Kognitionen – Modelle, Theorien, Methoden, Anwendung [The development of social cognition: Models, theories, applications]* (pp. 65–131). Stuttgart: Klett-Cotta.

Foot, P. (1972). Morality as a system of hypothetical imperatives. *Philosophical Review, 81*, 305–316.

Gibbs, J. C. (2003). *Moral development and reality: Beyond the theories of Kohlberg and Hoffman*. Thousand Oaks, CA: Sage.

Haidt, J. (2001). The emotional dog and its rational tail: A social intuitionist approach to moral judgment. *Psychological Review, 108*, 814–834.

Hannaford, R. V. (1985). Moral reasoning and action in young children. *The Journal of Value Inquiry, 19*, 85–98.

Homann, K. (2004). Braucht die Wirtschaftsethik eine "moralische Motivation"? [Does business and economics ethics need "moral motivation"?] In V. Arnold (Ed.), *Wirtschaftsethische Perspektiven VII – Methodische Grundsatzfragen, Unternehmensethik, Verteilungsfragen, Gentechnik und Fragen der medizinischen Ethik [Perspectives of business and economics ethics VII: Fundamental methodological questions, business ethics, questions of distribution, biotechnological and medical ethics.]* (pp. 33–60). Berlin: Duncker & Humblot.

Keller, M., Lourenço, O., Malti, T., & Saalbach, H. (2003). The multifaceted phenomenon of "happy victimizers": A cross-cultural comparison of moral emotions. *British Journal of Developmental Psychology, 21*, 1–18.

Kochanska, G. (1993). Toward a synthesis of parental socialization and child temperament in early development of conscience. *Child Development, 64*, 325–347.

Kohlberg, L., & Candee, D. (1984). The relationship of moral judgment to moral action. In L. Kohlberg, *Essays on moral development: Vol. II. The psychology of moral development* (pp. 498–581). San Francisco: Harper and Row.

Kohlberg, L., & Kramer, R. (1969). Continuities and discontinuities in childhood and adult moral development. *Human Development, 12,* 93–120.

Krettenauer, T., Malti, T., & Sokol, B. (2008). The development of moral emotion expectancies and the happy victimizer phenomenon: A critical review of theory and application. *European Journal of Developmental Science, 2,* 221–235.

Lagattuta, K. H. (2005). When you shouldn't do what you want to do: Young children's understanding of desires, rules, and emotions. *Child Development, 76,* 713–733.

Lourenço, O. (1997). Children's attributions of moral emotions to victimizers: Some data, doubts, and suggestions. *British Journal of Developmental Psychology, 15,* 425–438.

Mackie, J. L. (1977). *Ethics: Inventing right and wrong*. Harmondsworth: Penguin.

Malti, T., Gummerum, M., Keller, M., & Buchmann, M. (2009). Children's moral motivation, sympathy, and prosocial behavior. *Child Development, 80,* 442–460.

Malti, T., & Latzko, B. (2010). Children's moral emotions and moral condition: Towards an integrative perspective. In B. Latzko & T. Malti (Eds.), *Children's Moral Emotions and Moral Cognition: Developmental and Educational Perspectives. New Directions for Child and Adolescent Development*, *129*, 1–10.

Minnameier, G (2000). Strukturgenese moralischen Denkens – Eine Rekonstruktion der Piagetschen Entwicklungslogik und ihre moraltheoretischen Folgen [*structural genesis of moral thinking – reconstructing Piagetian developmental logic and its consequences for moral theory*]. Münster: Waxmann.

Minnameier, G. (2001). A new "stairway to moral heaven"? A systematic reconstruction of stages of moral thinking based on a Piagetian "logic" of cognitive development. *Journal of Moral Education, 30,* 317–337.

Minnameier, G. (2004). Peirce-suit of truth: Why inference to the best explanation and abduction ought not to be confused. *Erkenntnis, 60,* 75–105.

Minnameier, G. (2005). Developmental progress in ancient Greek ethics. *European Journal of Developmental Psychology, 2,* 2005, 71–99.

Minnameier, G. (2009). Measuring moral progress: A neo-Kohlbergian approach and two case studies. *Journal of Adult Development, 16,* 131–143.

Minnameier, G. (2010). Entwicklung moralischen Denkens [Development of moral judgment]. In B. Latzko & T. Malti (Eds.), *Moralentwicklung und -erziehung in Kindheit und Adoleszenz* [*Moral development and education in childhood and adolescence*]. (pp. 47–67). Göttingen: Hogrefe.

Narvaez, D., & Rest, J. (1995). The four components of acting morally. In W. M. Kurtines & J. L. Gewirtz (Eds.), *Moral development: An introduction* (pp. 385–399). Boston: Allyn & Bacon.

Nunner-Winkler, G. (1993). Die Entwicklung moralischer Motivation [Development of moral motivation]. In W. Edelstein, G. Nunner-Winkler, & G. Noam (Eds.), *Moral und Person [The moral self]* (pp. 278–303). Frankfurt/Main: Suhrkamp.

Nunner-Winkler, G. (1999). Development of moral understanding and moral motivation. In F. E. Weinert & W. Schneider (Eds.), *Individual development from 3 to 12* (pp. 253–292). Cambridge, UK: Cambridge University Press.

Nunner-Winkler, G. (2007). Development of moral motivation from childhood to early adulthood. *Journal of Moral Education, 36*, 399–414.

Nunner-Winkler, G., & Sodian, B. (1988). Children's understanding of moral emotions. *Child Development, 59*, 1323–1338.

Oser, F. (1999). Die mißachtete Freiheit moralischer Alternativen: Urteile über Handeln, Handeln ohne Urteile [The unconsidered freedom of moral alternatives: Judgments about actions, actions without judgments]. In D. Garz, F. Oser, & W. Althof (Eds.), *Moralisches Urteil und Handeln[Moral judement and moral action]* (pp. 168–219). Frankfurt/Main: Suhrkamp.

Piaget, J. (1977). *The moral judgement of the child.* Harmondsworth, UK: Penguin. (Original work published 1932)

Piaget, J., & Garcia, R. (1989). *Psychogenesis and the history of science.* New York: Columbia University Press.

Railton, P. (1986). Moral realism. *The Philosophical Review, 95*, 163–207.

Rest, J. R. (1983). Morality. In J. H. Flavell & E. M. Markman (Series Eds.) and P. H. Mussen (Vol. Ed.), *Handbook of child psychology: Vol. III. Cognitive development* (4th ed., pp. 556–629). New York: Wiley.

Rest, J. R. (1984). The major components of morality. In W. M. Kurtinez & J. L. Gewirtz (Eds.), *Morality, moral behavior, and moral development* (pp. 24–38). New York: Wiley.

Rest, J., Narvaez, D., Bebeau, M. J., & Thoma, S. J. (1999). *Postconventional moral thinking: A neo-Kohlbergian approach*. Mahwah, NJ: Erlbaum.

Sayre-McCord, G. (1997). The metaethical problem: A discussion of Michael Smith's "The Moral Problem." *Ethics, 108*, 55–83.

Smith, M. (1997). In defence of the moral problem. *Ethics, 108*, 84–119.

Smith, M. (2005). *The moral problem.* Oxford: Blackwell. (Original work published 1994)

Smith, M. (2008). The truth about internalism. In W. Sinnott-Armstrong (Ed.), *Moral psychology: Vol. 3. The neuroscience of morality: Emotion, brain disorders, and development* (pp. 207–215). Cambridge, MA: MIT Press.

Sokol, B. (2007, November). *Moral emotions in middle childhood: Foundations for the development of the moral self.* Paper presented at the Association of Moral Education, New York.

Thoma, S. (1994). Moral judgments and moral action. In J. R. Rest & D. Narváez (Eds.), *Moral development in the professions: Psychology and applied ethics* (pp. 199–211). Hillsdale, NJ: Erlbaum.

Turiel, E. (1998). The development of morality. In W. Damon (Series Ed.) & N. Eisenberg (Vol. Ed.), *Handbook of child psychology: Vol. 3. Social, emotional, and personality development* (5th ed., pp. 863–932). New York: Wiley.

Zangwill, N. (2003). Externalist moral motivation. *American Philosophical Quarterly, 40*, 143–154.

GERHARD MINNAMEIER is professor of vocational and business education at the RWTH Aachen University, Germany. E-mail: minnameier@lbw.rwth-aachen.de, Web page: www.lbw.rwth-aachen.de.

Narvaez, D. (2010). The emotional foundations of high moral intelligence. In B. Latzko & T. Malti (Eds.), *Children's moral emotions and moral cognition: Developmental and educational perspectives. New Directions for Child and Adolescent Development*, 129, 77–94. San Francisco: Jossey-Bass.

5

The Emotional Foundations of High Moral Intelligence

Darcia Narvaez

Abstract

Moral intelligence is grounded in emotion and reason. Neuroscientific and clinical research illustrate how early life co-regulation with caregivers influences emotion, cognition, and moral character. Triune ethics theory (Narvaez, 2008) integrates neuroscientific, evolutionary, and developmental findings to explain differences in moral functioning, identifying security, engagement, and imagination ethics that can be dispositionally fostered by experience during sensitive periods, but also situationally triggered. Mature moral functioning relies on the integration of emotion, intuition, and reasoning, which come together in adaptive ethical expertise. Moral expertise can be cultivated in organizations using the integrative ethical education model. © Wiley Periodicals, Inc.

Moral theory was much simpler when the human was viewed as a mind-spirit caged in a body wracked by passions (Plato's view). Morality came about through the development of reasoning as a means to control those wayward emotions. Similarly, there was a long tradition of viewing the human as an inherently selfish (and sinful) creature (Augustine's view). Accordingly, morality developed through a painstaking process of punishment and coercive training of good habits. Both approaches adopted a dualistic view: that mind and body, reason and emotion, are separate and separable. Although such views still infuse popular and academic approaches to parenting, education, and moral development theory, these perspectives no longer stand the tests of empirical science.

First, although imagination and other deliberate processes affect moral functioning (like "dangerous ideas," Eidelson & Eidelson, 2003), the dominance of reasoning in behavior is undermined by empirical evidence showing that much of behavior is initiated before conscious thought or decision (e.g., Bargh & Ferguson, 2000; Libet, 1985). Second, although individuals cannot help but use the self as the base for perception and action, anthropological and primate research offer convincing evidence for long histories of social cooperation and altruism in human and other species (for reviews, see de Waal, 1988, 2009; Fry, 2006). Thus the premises of dualistic views appear to be flawed. The emerging view is that character or personality is rooted in emotion systems shaped by enactive interaction with the social world early in life (Greenspan & Shanker, 2004; Schore, 1994) and influenced by social experience throughout life (Cacioppo & Patrick, 2008). These and other new understandings suggest that a much more complicated moral theory is needed. A new theory should take into account how understanding is grounded in physical experience (Lakoff & Johnson, 1999) and, most importantly for this chapter, how particular lived experience early in life builds and wires the infant brain for later functioning. Early life may establish an optimal or a suboptimal trajectory for emotional and moral intelligence (e.g., Crabbe & Phillips, 2003; Schore, 1994). This chapter examines the roots of morality in early experience, the embodied nature of moral learning, and the importance of emotional social experience for moral functioning throughout life.

Early Experience Shapes Affective-Moral Systems

The profound and malleable influence of early experience has been implicated in cognitive, emotional, and moral development at least since mid-twentieth century when first Hartman (1964) then Bowlby (1951, 1988) alerted psychologists to its importance. Bowlby postulated the "environment of evolutionary adaptedness" (EEA) as formative for brain development. More recently, anthropologists have identified many of the critical characteristics of the EEA for infants and young children (see Hewlett &

Lamb, 2005, for a review). These match up with mammalian ape needs generally and include breastfeeding two to five years, nearly constant touch in the first years of life, prompt response to fusses and cries, multiage play groups, and multiple adult caregivers. All of these elements contribute to optimal physical and emotion development (see Narvaez, Panksepp, Schore, & Gleason, in press, for a review), influencing personality dispositions and moral functioning (see Narvaez, 2008, for a review).

More recently, neuroscientific and clinical research paradigms have been able to illustrate how early life construction and "tuning up" of emotion systems influences character (Cozolino, 2006; Schore, 1994, 2001; Siegel, 1999). By "character," I mean the person-by-context patterned or habitual responses, developed from life experience, that a person brings to a situation. First, as demonstrated by numerous animal experiments, early experience establishes the structure and functioning of the mammalian brain and body systems (e.g., Harlow, 1986; Meaney, 2001). This has been often characterized as "attachment" (Bowlby, 1951), a term that does not capture how integral early experience is to all of functioning. For example, maternal responsiveness, a key component of "attachment parenting," is related to vagal nerve establishment. The vagus nerve, part of the parasympathetic nervous system, is related to all sorts of body systems including cardiac, digestive, respiratory, as well as moral (e.g., Donzella, Gunnar, Krueger, & Alwin, 2000; Propper et al., 2008; Stam, Akkermans, & Wiegant, 1997). Non-responsive parenting is related to poor vagal tone (e.g., Calkins, Smith, Gill, & Johnson, 1998; Porter, 2003). Vagal tone is related to feelings of compassion (Eisenberg & Eggum, 2008, for a review).The intersubjectivity and mutual co-regulation with caregivers set up the neuroendocrinological systems that underlie emotional functioning. "Development may be conceptualized as the transformation of external into internal regulation" where the "progression represents an increase of complexity of the maturing brain systems that adaptively regulate the interaction between the developing organism and the social environment" (Schore, 2001, p. 202). For example, maternal touch can lower an infant's heart rate during a distressing experience, helping the child form a more adaptive response to stress (Calkins & Hill, 2007). On the other hand, when separated, a mother's absence can cause stress hormone release and disruption in multiple physiological systems in the offspring (Hofer, 1987, 1994; Polan & Hofer, 1999). In primates, chronic distress is related to a permanent change in brain stress response systems towards oversensitivity and overreactivity (Anisman Zaharia, Meaney, & Merali, 1998), leading to multiple health problems (e.g., diabetes, hypertension, depression; Chrousos & Gold, 1992). Stress response reactivity influences emotion and cognitive development and, hence, the functioning of character. A person in personal distress is less likely to be able to focus on others.

Not only does parenting influence the structure and wiring of physical and psychological systems, it effects epigenetic change on hundreds of genes, one of which has been mapped by Michael Meaney and his lab. Using rats, Meaney and colleagues (Weaver, Szyf, & Meaney, 2002) have demonstrated that high nurturing maternal behavior during a critical period in early life turns on a receptor gene that encodes glucocorticoid receptor protein, critical for alleviating distress. Low nurturing mothers (low-licking) do not turn on the receptor gene in their offspring, who go on to have elevated stress responses for the rest of their lives. Cross-fostering studies show that the effect is environmental and not genetic; experience influences gene expression ("epigenetics;" Crabbe & Phillips, 2003; Francis, Diorio, Liu, & Meaney, 1999). The same neurological differences have been demonstrated in human adults who had been abused as children and committed suicide (McGowan et al., 2009).

Emotion underlies cognition and guides behavior generally (Greenspan, 1979). Emotions "give birth" to the ability to think and invent symbols (Greenspan & Shanker, 2004, p. 1). "Sensory and subjective experiences ... are the basis for creative and logical reflection" (p. 2). To develop symbolic thinking, humans must learn to transform basic emotions into increasingly complex emotional signaling in "reciprocal, co-regulated emotional interaction" with the caregiver (p. 30). As they co-regulate with a caregiver, children learn to self-regulate, one of the key components of successful development (Shonkoff & Phillips, 2000). The child signals intent and the sensitive caregiver responds to the intent, helping the child regulate strong or "catastrophic" emotions, before direct action is taken. The ability to signal back and forth solves problems that would otherwise result in direct action (e.g., biting when hungry). Emotional signaling eventually allows the separation of an image or desire from immediate action. Ideas are images that are invested with emotion, but have been set free from fixed or immediate action. Individuals who are unable to signal with their emotions act impulsively on their intense emotions, or engage in fragmented or polarized thinking. When emotional signaling is thwarted by factors like a depressed mother (or perhaps even by small cultural elements like the use of strollers that face away from the caregiver; Zeedyk, 2008), developmental delays may ensue (Tronick, 2007; Zuckerman, Bauchner, Parker, & Cabral, 1990).

In older normal children, it becomes more obvious that reflective thinking is grounded in "lived emotional experience" (Greenspan & Shanker, 2004, p. 233). Children with higher levels of social experience develop greater emotional self-awareness and are able to use emotions effectively to think out problems, showing superior social skills, moral reasoning, and intelligence. The children are able to create ideas *from experience* (i.e., play) and organize those ideas in a broader, analytical context—Greenspan and Shanker's definition of intelligence. Indeed, children's play is found to be a powerful educator of both emotions and cognition (Panksepp, 2007).

The early years of life form the foundations not only of general intelligence and social competence (Greenspan & Shanker, 2004), but also of moral functioning (Narvaez, 2008). Moral functioning refers to the propensities and capacities for response to events that affect the welfare of others near and far. Moral functioning emerges from conceptual knowledge about the world, particularly the social world as experienced, and from emotional knowledge—the way that the emotions have been tuned up to guide experience. In the shaping of emotions and concepts through everyday experience, moral propensities such as conscience development are formed in the intersubjectivity of child and caregiver (Kochanska, 2002; Thompson, 2009). Triune ethics theory describes several basic ways that moral functioning is influenced by the emotion and cognitive structures developed during sensitive periods.

Triune Ethics Theory

Triune ethics theory (TET; Narvaez, 2008, 2009) integrates neuroscientific, evolutionary, and developmental findings to explain differences in moral functioning (capacities that involve noticing, feeling for, imagining, solving, and acting on the needs of others). TET proposes that three basic types of affectively rooted moral orientations emerged from human evolution and are influenced by early care and social environments: the ethics of security, engagement, and imagination. Each orientation has neurobiological roots that are suggested by the structures and circuitry of human brain evolution (MacLean, 1990; Panksepp, 1998) and each prioritizes a different set of emotions. When the propensities for action in a particular orientation trump other values, they become an ethic. That is, as a type of motivated cognition, an activated ethic influences what affordances (action possibilities) are salient, and what goals and actions are preferred. Thus, moral action emerges from the affective stance underlying the ethic that imbues ongoing experience with a particular moral value (Moll et al., 2002). Each ethic makes normative claims, making particular actions seem "right" based on the interaction between the particular context and the habits of mind brought to the situation by the person (character).

Security Ethic: "Bunker" Morality. Evolutionarily older brain structures (extrapyramidal action nervous system; Panksepp, 1998) related to morality are activated when a person is threatened, such as the anger-rage emotion system rooted in the sympathetic system and the fear-distress emotion circuit rooted in the parasympathetic system. These are useful networks for self-preservation. However, when humans use these instincts habitually to determine behavior towards others, they are acting from the security ethic. Laboratory studies show that a security orientation is easily primed with evocations of death and other threats, leading to less compassion for others (e.g., Mikulincer, Shaver, Gillath, & Nitzberg, 2005). Priming with a market orientation (i.e., for money) also makes the security ethic more accessible and decreases compassion (see Aquino & Freeman, 2009, for a review).

The EEA characteristics noted above no longer pervade the early years of life (or any age) in the United States, suggesting that optimal prosocial emotion systems are not being nurtured (Narvaez, Panksepp, Schore, & Gleason, in press). Indeed, anxiety and depression exist in epidemic proportions across the country (U.S. Department of Health and Human Services, Substance Abuse and Mental Health Services Administration, 1999). Persons with suboptimal emotion systems will more easily trigger the security ethic when under stress. Personal distress becomes the dominant focus, making empathy towards others and compassionate response difficult (see Eisenberg & Eggum, 2008, for a review). Perception and action choices narrow to those related to "fight/flight" (Henry & Wang, 1998), and will opt to make moral decisions based on "what's good for me and mine" (personal interest schema; Rest, Narvaez, Bebau, & Thoma, 1999), lacking the perspective taking and empathy that underlie more advanced forms of moral reasoning. In fact, in recent research with the defining issues test, the personal interest schema (Kohlberg's Stages 2 and 3) is increasing among U.S. college students across the country while postconventional reasoning (Kohlberg's Stages 5 and 6) is decreasing (Chung, Bebeau, Thoma, & You, 2009).

Engagement Ethic: Harmony Morality. The ethic of engagement involves the emotional systems (the visceral-emotional nervous system on the hypothalamic-limbic axis; Panksepp, 1998) that allow for intimacy and "limbic resonance," mind-to-mind coordination vital for mammalian brain functioning (for a review, see Lewis, Amini, & Lannon, 2000). The ethic of engagement is oriented to face-to-face emotional affiliation with others, particularly through caring relationships and social bonds. The ethic of engagement underlies compassionate response and self-sacrifice for others. For example, moral exemplars are typically propelled by affiliation and compassion values when they take committed or risky action for others (Oliner & Oliner, 1988; Walker & Frimer, 2009). With an upbringing that more closely matches the EEA, the engagement ethic develops fully and leads to values of compassion and openness towards others (see Eisler & Levine, 2002, for a similar view). For example, children with responsive mothers are more likely to display early conscience development, agreeable personalities, and prosocial behavior (e.g., Kochanska, 2002), pointing to the importance of empathy development in the first years of life (Maxwell & DesRoches, this volume).

Imagination Ethic: Mindful or Heartless Morality. The imagination ethic is grounded in more recently evolved brain capacities (i.e., prefrontal cortex) that are shown to be fundamental for social and moral functioning in complex societies. The ethic of imagination uses humanity's fullest reasoning capacities to adapt to ongoing social relationships and to address concerns beyond the immediate. Unlike the ethics of security and engagement, the systems underlying the imagination ethic allow an individual to envision alternatives to what exists and make plans and guide action for change. However, the imagination ethic can be harnessed by either the security ethic—oriented to self/group protection against imagined outsiders and detached from empathy, creating a "heartless morality," or the engagement ethic—oriented to collaboration with imagined outsiders or future generations, a "mindful morality." Like the systems that underlie the engagement ethic, the prefrontal cortex is sensitive to environmental input early in development (Anderson, Bechara, Damasio, Tranel, & Damasio, 1999; Kodituwakku, Kalberg, & May, 2001) and late in development, such as emerging adulthood (Newman, Holden, & Delville, 2005). Triune ethics theory underscores the importance of early life in establishing brain structures and interconnections that allow for deep, compassionate relational commitment to others and the intellectual capacities for complex moral reasoning and perspective taking. Children's moral dispositions are formed by immersed social experience in combination with the cultural narratives that explain the experience (see Gutzwiller-Helfenfinger, Gasser, & Malti, this volume).

Development of Moral Functioning

Although early experience of secure attachment and mentoring can provide an advantage for adult psychological well-being (McAdams, 2009) and moral exemplarity (Walker & Frimer, 2009), brain plasticity and changing experience offer a chance to continuously build capacities for moral functioning. In other words, early life experience has a great impact on brain structures and wiring but is not all that "makes the man." Cognitive transformation occurs throughout life, and may be more influential during sensitive periods in life after childhood (e.g., early adolescence, late adolescence/emerging adulthood, psychotherapy).

Emotions form the foundations of brain functioning in terms of motivation and intelligence, but these are not enough for mature moral functioning. Although some have argued for the dominance of intuitive emotion for moral functioning (e.g., Haidt, 2001), much of intuitionist research has examined naïve or seat-of-the-pants intuition rather than educated or well-formed intuition (Narvaez, in press-b). Well-formed intuition, from deliberative practice in appropriate environments, relies on the conceptual structures that derive from experience. Novice-to-expert learning describes this process (Bransford, Cocking, & Brown, 1999).

Adaptive Ethical Expertise

Moral psychology has spent most of its time examining special cases of decision making (e.g., Heinz dilemma, trolley problems, eating dog). As a result we know very little about "everyday ethical coping" (Appiah, 2008; Dreyfus & Dreyfus, 1990). From his neuroscientific studies of patients with brain damage, Goldberg (2002) showed that there are two types of decision making, veridical and adaptive. In veridical decision making, the details of a scenario are prearranged. (e.g., what should Mary do [in this scenario I have devised for you?]). In adaptive decision making, the agent herself must try to make sense of the ongoing flow of information, a complex task that requires attending to and sorting stimuli, prioritizing, weighing actions and effects, plus a multitude of other executive functions. Some have called this the real work of moral functioning (Appiah, 2008), capacities for which vary among individuals based on expertise (Narvaez & Lapsley, 2005).

In most domains in life we can see a range of capacities that runs from novice to expert (Bransford et al., 1999; Sternberg, 1999). Expertise refers to a refined, deep understanding that is evident in practice and action. Experts and novices differ from one another in three basic ways. First, experts in a particular domain have more and better organized knowledge than novices (Chi, Glaser, & Farr, 1988; Sternberg, 1998). Expert knowledge is of several kinds that interact in performance: for example, declarative (what), procedural (how), and conditional (when and how much) knowledge. Second, experts perceive and react to the world differently, noticing details and opportunities that novices miss (Feltovich, Ford, & Hoffman, 1997; Johnson & Mervis, 1997). Third, experts behave differently. Whereas novices use conscious, effortful methods to solve problems, many expert skills are highly automatic and effortless (Feltovich, Prietula & Ericsson, 2006).

The notion of expertise development applies to the moral domain as well (Narvaez, 2005, 2006; Narvaez & Gleason, 2007). Paraphrasing the ideas of Aristotle and Mencius, Francisco Varela (1999) wrote: "a wise (or virtuous) person is *one who knows what is good and spontaneously does it*" (p. 4, emphasis added). In fact, moral exemplars often speak as if perception and action are linked (e.g., "what else could I do?" Monroe, 1994). Moral experts demonstrate holistic orientations in one or more psychological capacities (Narvaez & Rest, 1995; Rest, 1983). For example, experts in ethical sensitivity are better at quickly and accurately "reading" a moral situation and determining needs and potential responses. They are able to control personal bias in an effort to be morally responsive to others. Experts in ethical judgment are skilled at reasoning about duty and consequences and assessing which potential action is most moral for the situation. Experts in ethical focus cultivate ethical self-regulation and ethical self-reflection. They foster an ethical identity that fosters habituated ethical concern (Narvaez, in press-b). Experts in ethical action know how to marshal their courage to stay on task and take the necessary steps to get the ethical job done. Experts in a particular excellence have more and better organized knowledge about it, have highly tuned perceptual skills for it, have deep moral desire for it, and benefit from multiple automatized capacities. In short, they have more *content* knowledge and more *process* knowledge, more implicit and explicit conceptual and emotional knowledge (see Narvaez, 2006, for greater detail).

More recently, the education of children has been viewed as the development of expertise in each of many domains (Bransford et al., 1999). How does expertise come about? Experts in training have extensive, focused practice in particular contexts (Ericsson & Smith, 1991). They are immersed in the domain while at the same time are guided by someone with greater expertise who "whispers in the ear" about what to notice, what to practice, and how to act and why (e.g., Abernathy & Hamm, 1995). Good caregiving provides just such guidance in multiple domains, as is often seen with young children ("Where do we put our boots when we take them off?" "Why do we eat our vegetables before eating our dessert?"). But such guidance should cut across all ages and domains based not on age but level of expertise. Aristotle advocated having a mentor until the individual is able to mentor the self (Urmson, 1988). Thus, good intuitions, from immersion, are cultivated at the same time as conscious understanding, from explicit guidance. Expertise involves "reflexively activated, context-specific schemata" (Ritchhart & Perkins, 2005, p. 789) whose development requires more than the usual everyday amount of exposure to a domain, typically requiring thousands of hours of deliberate study (Ericsson, 2006; Ericsson & Charness, 1994).

Education for moral expertise fosters moral reasoning and moral intuitions simultaneously within particular contexts. Through the course of expertise training, perceptions are fine-tuned and developed into chronically accessed constructs (Lapsley & Lasky, 1999; Narvaez, Lapsley, Hagele, & Lasky, 2006); interpretive frameworks are learned and, with practice, applied automatically; action schemas are honed to high levels of automaticity (Hogarth, 2001). "Skills" or capacities form an embodied cognition (Varela, Thompson, & Rosch, 1991), a holistic and contextualized understanding that engages the entire brain–mind–body system. Virtues arise from immersed practice beginning with caregiver co-regulation early in life, which establishes trajectories for future functioning (Churchland, 1998; see Greenspan & Shanker, 2004, for a review). As for all of social life, emotional wherewithal underlies ethical expertise. But empathy alone is not enough either. Empathy without discipline is useless to those in need (Trout, 2009). With a set of deeply attuned knowledge and cultivated habits, experts "know what to do and do it," displaying a seamless interface between perception and committed action.

This adaptive ethical expertise approach fits with philosophies of multiple traditions. In emphasizing the foundational importance of emotion for moral functioning, emotivist theories are acknowledged. In advocating cultivation of deliberate processes like reasoning and reflection, the deontological and utilitarian theories are integrated. And in emphasizing the cultivation of ethical capacities from novice to expert functioning, virtue theory is highlighted. Virtue theory more holistically emphasizes multiple individual capacities or virtues (actionable understanding) as well as the relation of the individual to the community group. Dewey's pragmatism (see Fesmire, 2003, for a review) offers a similar holistic view of individual development within communal experience. As a result, both pragmatism and virtue theory may offer more psychologically veridical views of moral development (Casebeer, 2003, 2005; Churchland, 1998; Fesmire, 2003) than other theories, including the dualist theories mentioned at the beginning of this chapter.

Emotional and Ethical Expertise Development in Schools and Youth Organizations

When applied to the classroom, adaptive ethical expertise development and triune ethics theory suggest an integrative approach to cultivating moral character such as that described in the integrative ethical education model (IEE; partially developed under USDE OERI Grant # R215V980001). IEE takes into account the centrality of emotion in motivation and learning, emphasizing relationships, emotional signaling, adult guidance, personal autonomy, and self-actualization within the community.

Caring Relationship. Designing environments for children that match as much as possible the EEA is assumed to be optimal. This means that teachers ought to establish a secure relationship with each child. Sometimes this is difficult with children who have experienced poor caregiving or trauma in the past; but with patience and persistence, it can happen (Watson & Eckert, 2003). For an individual to be open to ongoing experience, their needs and individuality need to be acknowledged and taken into account. Just as within the parent-child relationship, the responsive teacher expresses openness to mutual influence and models "unconditional positive regard" (Rogers, 1983) for the child's "becoming" a prosocial member of the community. In such a relationship, the child can thrive as a person and as a student.

Supportive Climate. Climates or cultures comprise the practices and expectations shared by members of an organization. Learning climates vary, fostering different mindsets, perceptions, and habits towards school tasks. When students perceive teachers emphasizing performance (e.g., grades, competition), students are more likely to adopt performance goals themselves (looking good, or not looking bad; Urdan, Midgley, &

Anderman, 1998), whereas when students perceived teachers emphasizing understanding, they are more likely to adopt a mastery orientation to learning (Urdan & Midgley, 2001). A mastery orientation, regardless of performance orientation, is related to prosocial attitudes and reported behavior (Vaydich, Khmelkov, & Narvaez, 2007). Different social climates foster different attitudes towards self and others (DeVries & Zan, 1994). Caring community classrooms provide the support students need for achievement and prosocial behavior, as so well demonstrated by the Child Development Project (Battistich, 2008). A sustaining climate offers a caring mastery learning environment but also fosters human potential through intentional guidance for purposeful, democratic participation (see Narvaez, in press-a) where students care for one another's welfare (Power & Higgins-D'Alessandro, 2008).

Ethical Skills through a Novice-to-Expert Pedagogy. When teachers (and parents) view children with a growth mindset (instead of a fixed mindset; Dweck, 2006), they realize that students require structured guidance to foster development in a host of skills needed to live a good life (Lave, 1988). Children today often are isolated from adult life and lack good role models. Along with immersion in experience for developing intuition (Hogarth, 2001), deliberate, intentional instruction is required to foster moral problem-solving skills, which include social and emotional learning (Elias, Parker, Kash, Weissberg, & O'Brien, 2008).

The Minnesota Community Voices and Character Education project (Narvaez, Bock, Endicott, & Lies, 2004) identified sets of ethical skills that can be taught in public schools. Using the novice-to-expert approach described above, the teacher provides guidance at each of four levels of novice-to-expert instruction. The example of emotion regulation is used here as an illustration. In level one, immersion, the teacher provides multiple examples of capable skill performance at developmentally appropriate levels. The teacher could demonstrate emotion regulation or show story characters who successfully regulated emotion (in ways appropriate for their culture and age). Students learn to attend to the "big picture" of the skill domain (e.g., noticing that a particular emotion was being regulated). Sometimes, anti-heroes (the opposite of exemplary performance) are useful in illustrating the importance of the skill. So the teacher might also show examples of poor self-regulation. In level two, the educator draws attention to particular subskills that the students can practice in class. Students might practice counting to ten and other skills for when they get upset. In level three, practice procedures, the teacher models skill sets (e.g., while thinking aloud) and students practice in role play and in actual everyday situations (e.g., counting to ten when they get upset in class). Students help one another remember the steps to take. In level four, integrating learning across contexts, the educator sets up ways for students to practice problem solving in multiple settings, to learn how to adjust skill application to different situations. Students could practice counting to ten on the playground, at home, in the cafeteria, and keep a journal of their success.

Fostering Self-Authorship. Autonomy is a fundamental characteristic of intellectual and moral maturity (Piaget, 1932) and is particularly important for moral functioning (Narvaez, in press-b). Moral self-authorship capacities include executive functioning capacities like moral self-monitoring (Am I taking all sides into account in making my decision?) and moral self-reflection (Does this action align with my moral identity?). Those with good self-monitoring are able, for example, to change strategies when a particular course of action is not working, whether working a math problem or a moral problem.

Restoring the Ecological System of Support. Reinvigorating and coordinating the child's network of support among family, community, and neighborhood institutions means that each area aligns goals to build assets and foster flourishing in the child and neighborhood (Lerner, Dowling, & Anderson, 2003). It is in the community that children and youth practice and apply ethical competencies. After all, moral development is about learning for life (Dewey, 1938). Each community has its own approach to moral character and must be engaged in fostering the flourishing of the young.

Mature Moral Functioning

Moral self-authorship continues throughout life and extends into the deepening of a moral self-identity. As described more fully elsewhere (Blasi, 2009; Narvaez, in press-b), mature moral functioning involves the interplay of emotions, intuitions, and reasoning in moral imagination, along with committed empathic concern, and metacognitive skills such as moral self-regulation, moral self-reflection, and moral locus of control, among other developed capacities.

Conclusion

Moral structures are shaped, like all embodied structures, by early experience. Newer understandings of mammalian needs and the environment of evolutionary adaptedness suggest ways to foster optimal human and moral development. Current societal child-rearing policies and practices for early life do not match what humans need for flourishing (see Narvaez & Panksepp, 2009). The view here is that these suboptimal environments are fostering a more primitive type of morality, the security ethic, which predominates in environments of extreme social stress. In these environments humans look like they are naturally violent. Nevertheless, in circumstances of social support, our ancestors were largely peaceful and cooperative (Fry, 2006), an orientation that is more visible among the populace during natural disasters when individuals typically go out of their way to help others at personal cost (Solnit, 2009).

From birth, learning best takes place through immersion in supportive environments with guidance from more-experienced mentors. In moral development, the caregivers first provide the relational environment that wires the brain for sociality. Ideally, early experience provides a responsive, co-regulating structure that fosters deep pleasure in sociality. The brain is a pleasure machine and will find ways to get pleasure from experience. For optimal moral functioning, it may be best to learn the ways of our ancestors—to foster pleasure from enjoyable relationships (Fry, 2006). The engagement ethic builds on pleasure from social relationships and in conjunction with the imagination ethic can be a powerful force for prosocial behavior. Thus, the view here is that if we pay attention to what human mammals need for optimal moral functioning, providing environments that foster intimate social relations and cultural narratives for the ethics of engagement and imagination, we may be able to reach peaceful co-existence again.

References

Abernathy, C. M., & Hamm, R. M. (1995). *Surgical intuition.* Philadephia: Hanley & Belfus.

Anderson, S. W., Bechara, A., Damasio, H., Tranel, D., & Damasio, A. R. (1999). Impairment of social and moral behavior related to early damage in human prefrontal cortex. *Nature Neuroscience*, 2, 1032–1037.

Anisman, H., Zaharia, M. D., Meaney, M. J., & Merali, Z. (1998). Do early-life events permanently alter behavioral and hormonal responses to stressors? *International Journal of Developmental Neuroscience, 16*(3–4), 149–164.

Appiah, K. (2008). *Experiments in ethics.* Cambridge, MA: Harvard University Press.

Aquino, K., & Freeman, D. (2009). Moral identity in business situations: A social-cognitive framework for understanding moral functioning. In D. Narvaez & D. K. Lapsley (Eds.), *Personality, identity, and character explorations in moral psychology* (pp. 375–395). New York: Cambridge University Press.

Bargh, J. A., & Ferguson, M. J. (2000). Beyond behaviorism: On the automaticity of higher mental processes. *Psychological Bulletin, 126*(6), 925–945.

Battistich, V. A. (2008). The Child Development Project: Creating caring school communities. In L.P. Nucci, & D. Narvaez (Eds.), *Handbook of moral and character education* (pp. 328–351). New York: Routledge.

Blasi, A. (2009). Moral reasoning and the moral functioning of mature adults. In D. Narvaez & D. K. Lapsley (Eds.), *Moral personality, identity and character: An interdisciplinary future* (pp. 396–440). New York: Cambridge University Press.

Bowlby, J. (1951). *Maternal care and mental health.* New York: Schocken.

Bowlby, J. (1988). *A secure base: Parent–child attachment and healthy human development.* New York: Basic Books.

Bransford, J. D., Brown, A. L., & Cocking, R. R. (Eds.). (1999). *How people learn: Brain, mind, experience, and school.* Washington, DC: National Academy Press.

Cacioppo, J. T., & Patrick, W. (2008). *Loneliness: Human nature and the need for social connection.* New York: W. W. Norton.

Calkins, S. D., & Hill, A. (2007). The emergence of emotion regulation: Biological and behavioural transactions in early development. In J. Gross & R. Thompson (Eds.), *The Handbook of emotion regulation* (pp. 229–248). New York: Guilford Press.

Calkins, S. D., Smith, C. L., Gill, K. L., & Johnson, M. C. (1998). Maternal interactive style across contexts: Relations to emotional, behavioral and physiological regulation during toddlerhood. *Social Development, 7*(3), 350–369.

Casebeer, W. D. (2003). *Natural ethical facts: Evolution, connectionism, and moral cognition* Cambridge, MA: MIT Press.

Casebeer, W. D. (2005). Neurobiology supports virtue theory on the role of heuristics in moral cognition. *Behavioral and Brain Sciences, 28*, 547–548.

Chi, M. T. H., Glaser, R., & Farr, M. J. (1988). *The nature of expertise*. Hillsdale, NJ: Erlbaum.

Chrousos, G. P., & Gold, P. W. (1992). The concepts of stress and stress system disorders: Overview of physical and behavioral homeostasis. *Journal of the American Medical Association, 267*(9), 1244–1252.

Chung, C.-T., Bebeau, M. J., Thoma, S. J., & You, D. (2009, April). *DIT-2: Moral schema norms—the updates from recent data sets*. Paper presented at the American Educational Research Association Annual Meeting, San Diego.

Churchland, P. (1998). Toward a cognitive neurobiology of the emotions. *Topoi, 17*, 83–96.

Cozolino, L. (2006). *The neuroscience of human relationships*. New York: W.W. Norton.

Crabbe, J. C., & Phillips, T. J. (2003). Mother nature meets mother nurture. *Nature Neuroscience, 6*, 440–442.

DeVries, R., & Zan, B. (1994). *Moral classrooms, moral children: Creating a constructivist atmosphere in early education*. New York: Teachers College Press.

de Waal, F. B. (1988). The communicative repertoire of captive bonobos (*pan paniscus*) compared to that of chimpanzees. *Behaviour, 106*, 183–251.

de Waal, F. B. (2009). The age of empathy. Nature's lessons for a kinder society. New York : Harmony Books.

Dewey, J. (1938). *Experience & education*. New York: Simon & Schuster.

Donzella, B., Gunnar, M. R., Krueger, W. K., & Alwin, J. (2000). Cortisol and vagal tone responses to competitive challenge in preschoolers: Associations with temperament. *Development Psychobiology*, 37(4), 209–220.

Dreyfus, H. L, & Dreyfus, S. E. (1990). What is moral maturity? A phenomenological account of the development of ethical expertise. In D. Rasmussen (Ed.), *Universalism vs. communitarianism*. Boston: MIT Press.

Dweck, C. (2006). *Mindset*. New York: Random House.

Eidelson, R. J., & Eidelson, J. I. (2003). Dangerous ideas: Five beliefs that propel groups toward conflict. *American Psychologist, 58*, 182-192.

Eisenberg, N., & Eggum, N. D. (2008). Empathic responding: Sympathy and personal distress. In B. Sullivan, M. Snyder, & J. Sullivan (Eds.), *Cooperation: The political psychology of effective human interaction*. Malden, MA: Blackwell Publishing.

Eisler, R., & Levine, D. S. (2002). Nurture, nature, and caring: We are not prisoners of our genes. *Brain and Mind, 3*, 9–52.

Elias, M. J., Parker, S. J., Kash, V. M., Weissberg, R. P., & O'Brien, M. U. (2008). Social and emotional learning, moral education, and character education: A comparative analysis and a view toward convergence. In L. P. Nucci & D. Narvaez (Eds.), *Handbook of moral and character education* (pp. 248–266). New York: Routledge.

Ericsson, K. A. (2006). The influence of experience and deliberate practice on the development of superior expert performance. In K. A. Ericsson, N. Charness, P. J. Feltovich, R. R. Hoffman (Eds.), *The Cambridge handbook of expertise and expert performance* (pp. 683–704). New York: Cambridge University Press.

Ericsson, K. A., & Charness, N. (1994). Expert performance: Its structure and acquisition. *American Psychologist, 49*, 725–747.

Ericsson, K. A., & Smith, J. (1991). *Toward a general theory of expertise*. New York: Cambridge University Press.

Feltovich, P. J., Ford, K. M., & Hoffman, R. R. (1997). *Expertise in context.* Cambridge, MA: MIT Press.

Feltovich, P. J., Prietula, N. H, & Ericsson, K. A. (2006). Studies of expertise from psychological perspectives. In K. A. Ericsson, N. Charness, P. J. Feltovich, R. R. Hoffman (Eds.), *The Cambridge handbook of expertise and expert performance* (pp. 41–68). New York: Cambridge University Press.

Fesmire, S. (2003). *John Dewey and moral imagination.* Bloomington: Indiana University Press.

Francis, D., Diorio, J., Liu, D., & Meaney, M. J. (1999). Nongenomic transmission across generations of maternal behavior and stress responses in the rat. *Science, 286*, 1155-1158.

Fry, D. P. (2006). *The human potential for peace: An anthropological challenge to assumptions about war and violence.* New York: Oxford University Press.

Goldberg, E. (2002). *The executive brain: Frontal lobes and the civilized brain.* New York: Oxford University Press.

Greenspan, S. I. (1979). Intelligence and adaptation: An integration of psychoanalytic and Piagetian developmental psychology. *Psychological Issues, 12*(3–4), 1–408.

Greenspan, S. I., & Shanker, S. I. (2004). *The first idea.* Cambridge, MA: Da Capo Press.

Gutzwiller-Helfenfinger, E., Gasser, L., & Malti, T. (2010). Moral emotions and moral judgments in children's narratives: Comparing real-life and hypothetical transgressions. In B. Latzko & T. Malti (Eds.), *Children's moral emotions and moral cognition: Developmental and educational perspectives. New Directions for Child and Adolescent Development, 129*, 11–31.

Haidt, J. (2001). The emotional dog and its rational tail: A social intuitionist approach to moral judgment. *Psychological Review, 108*, 814–834.

Harlow, H. (1986). *From learning to love.* New York: Praeger.

Hartman, H. (1964). *Essays on ego psychology.* New York: International Universities Press. (Original work published 1939)

Henry, J. P., & Wang, S. (1998). Effects of early stress on adult affiliative behavior, *Psychoneuroendocrinology, 23*(8), 863–875.

Hewlett, B. S., & Lamb, M. E. (2005). *Hunter-gatherer childhoods: Evolutionary, developmental and cultural perspectives.* New Brunswick, NJ: Aldine.

Hofer, M. A. (1987). Early social relationships as regulators of infant physiology and behavior. *Child Development, 58*(3), 633–647.

Hofer, M. A. (1994). Hidden regulators in attachment, separation, and loss. In N. A. Fox (Ed.), Emotion regulation: Behavioral and biological considerations. *Monographs of the Society for Research in Child Development, 59*, 192–207.

Hogarth, R. M. (2001). *Educating intuition.* Chicago: University of Chicago Press.

Johnson, K. E., & Mervis, C. B. (1997). Effects of varying levels of expertise on the basic level of categorization. *Journal of Experimental Psychology: General, 126*(3), 248–277.

Kochanska, G. (2002). Mutually responsive orientation between mothers and their young children: A context for the early development of conscience. *Current Directions in Psychological Science, 11*, 191–195.

Kodituwakku, P. W., Kalberg, W., & May, P. A. (2001). *Effects of prenatal alcohol exposure on executive functioning. Alcohol research and health: Alcohol-related birth defects: An update*, 25(3). Retrieved July 15, 2010, from http://pubs.niaaa.nih.gov/publications/social/Module10KFetaExposure/Module10K.html

Lakoff, G., & M. Johnson (1999). *Philosophy in the flesh: The embodied mind and its challenge to western thought.* New York: Basic Books.

Lapsley, D. K., & Hill, P. (2009). The social cognitive development of moral character. In D. Narvaez & D. K. Lapsley (Eds.). *Moral personality, identity and character: An interdisciplinary future* (pp. 185–213). New York: Cambridge University Press.

Lapsley, D. K., & Lasky, B. (1999). Prototypic moral character. *Identity, 1*(4), 345–363.

Lave, J. (1988). *Cognition in practice.* Hillsdale, NJ: Erlbaum.

Lerner, R. M., Dowling, E. M., & Anderson, P. M. (2003). Positive youth development: Thriving as a basis of personhood and civil society. *Applied Developmental Science,* 7(3), 172–180.

Lewis, T., Amini, F., & Lannon, R. (2000). *A general theory of love.* New York: Vintage.

Libet, B. (1985). Unconscious cerebral initiative and the role of conscious will involuntary action. *Behavioral and Brain Sciences, 8*, 529–566.

MacLean, P. D. (1990). *The triune brain in evolution: Role in paleocerebral functions.* New York: Plenum.

Maxwell, B., & DesRoches, S. (2010). Empathy and social-emotional learning: Pitfalls and touchstones for school-based programs. In B. Latzko & T. Malti (Eds.), *Children's moral emotions and moral cognition: Developmental and educational perspectives. New Directions for Child and Adolescent Development, 129*, 33–53.

McAdams, D. (2009). The moral personality. In D. Narvaez & D. K. Lapsley (Eds.), *Moral personality, identity and character: An interdisciplinary future* (pp. 11–29). New York: Cambridge University Press.

McGowan, P. O., Sasaki, A., D'Alessio, A. C., Dymov, S., Labonté, B., Szyf, M., et al. (2009). Epigenetic regulation of the glucocorticoid receptor in human brain associates with childhood abuse. *Nature Neuroscience, 12*, 342–348.

Meaney, M. J. (2001). Maternal care, gene expression, and the transmission of individual differences in stress reactivity across generations. *Annual Review of Neuroscience, 24*, 1161–1192.

Mikulincer, M., Shaver, P. R., Gillath, O., & Nitzberg, R. A. (2005). Attachment, caregiving, and altruism: Boosting attachment security increases compassion and helping. *Journal of Personality and Social Psychology, 89*(5), 817–839.

Moll, J., de Oliveira-Souza, R., Eslinger, P. J., Bramati, I. E., Mourao-Miranda, J., Andreiulo, P. A., et al. (2002). The neural correlates of moral sensitivity: A functional magnetic resonance imaging investigation of basic and moral emotions. *Journal of Neuroscience, 22*, 2730–2736.

Monroe, L. (1994). But what else could I do? Choice, identity and a cognitive-perceptual theory of ethical political behavior. *Political Psychology, 15*, 201–226.

Narvaez, D. (2006). Integrative ethical education. In M. Killen & J. Smetana (Eds.), *Handbook of moral development* (pp. 703–733). Mahwah, NJ: Erlbaum.

Narvaez, D. (2008). Triune ethics: The neurobiological roots of our multiple moralities. *New Ideas in Psychology, 26*, 95–119.

Narvaez, D. (2009). Triune Ethics Theory and moral personality. In D. Narvaez & D. K. Lapsley (Eds.), *Moral personality, identity and character: An interdisciplinary future* (pp. 136–158). New York: Cambridge University Press.

Narvaez, D. (in press-a). Building a sustaining classroom climate for purposeful ethical citizenship. In T. Lovat & R. Toomey (Eds.), *Handbook of values education and student wellbeing.* New York: Springer.

Narvaez, D. (in press-b). Moral complexity: The fatal attraction of truthiness and the importance of mature moral functioning. *Perspectives on Psychological Science.*

Narvaez, D., Bock, T., Endicott, L., & Lies, J. (2004). Minnesota's Community Voices and Character Education Project. *Journal of Research in Character Education*, 2, 89–112.

Narvaez, D., & Gleason, T. (2007). The influence of moral judgment development and moral experience on comprehension of moral narratives and expository texts. *The Journal of Genetic Psychology, 168*(3), 251–276.

Narvaez, D., & Lapsley, D. (2005). The psychological foundations of everyday morality and moral expertise. In D. Lapsley & C. Power (Eds.), *Character psychology and character education* (pp. 140–165). Notre Dame, IN: University of Notre Dame Press.

Narvaez, D., Lapsley, D. K., Hagele, S., & Lasky, B. (2006). Moral chronicity and social information processing: Tests of a social cognitive approach to the moral personality. *Journal of Research in Personality*, *40*, 966–985.

Narvaez, D., Panksepp, J., Schore, A., & Gleason, T. (Eds.) (in press). *Human nature, early experience and the environment of evolutionary adaptedness*. New York: Oxford University Press.

Narvaez, D., & Rest, J. (1995). The four components of acting morally. In W. Kurtines & J. Gewirtz (Eds.), *Moral behavior and moral development: An introduction* (pp. 385–400). New York: McGraw-Hill.

Newman, M. L., Holden, G. W., & Delville, Y. (2005). Isolation and the stress of being bullied. *Journal of Adolescence, 28*, 343–357.

Oliner, S. P., & Oliner, P. M. (1988). *The altruistic personality: Rescuers of Jews in Nazi Europe*. New York: Free Press.

Panksepp, J. (1998). *Affective neuroscience: The foundations of human and animal emotions*. New York: Oxford University Press.

Panksepp, J. (2007). Can PLAY diminish ADHD and facilitate the construction of the social brain. *Journal of the Canadian Academy of Child and Adolescent Psychiatry, 10*, 57–66.

Piaget, J. (1965). *The moral judgment of the child* (M. Gabain, Trans.). New York: Free Press. (Original work published 1932)

Polan, H. J., & Hofer, M. (1999). Psychological origins of infant attachment and separation responses. In J. Cassidy & P. R. Shaver (Eds.), *Handbook of Attachment* (pp. 162–180). New York: Guliford Press.

Porter, C. L. (2003). Coregulation in mother–infant dyads: Links to infants' cardiac vagal tone. Psychological Reports, 92, 307–319.

Power, F. C., & Higgins–D'Alessandro, A. (2008). The just community approach to moral education and the moral atmosphere of the school. In L. P. Nucci & D. Narvaez (Eds.), *Handbook of moral and character education* (pp. 230–247). New York: Routledge.

Propper, C., Moore, G. A., Mills-Koonce, W. R., Halpern, C. T., Hill-Soderlund, A. L., Calkins, S. D., et al. (2008). Gene–environment contributions to the development of infant vagal reactivity: The Interaction of dopamine and maternal sensitivity. *Child Development, 79*(5), 1377–1394.

Rest, J. (1983). Morality. In J. Flavell & E. Markham (Series Eds.) and P. Mussen (Vol. Ed.), *Manual of child psychology: Vol. 3. Cognitive development* (pp. 556–629). New York: Wiley.

Rest, J., Narvaez, D., Bebau, M. J., & Thoma, S. J. (1999). *Postconventional moral thinking: A neo-Kohlbergian approach*. Mahaw, N.J.: Lawrence Erlbaum Associates.

Ritchhart, R., & Perkins, D. N. (2005). Learning to think: The challenges of teaching thinking. In K. J. Holyoak & R. G. Morrison (Eds.), *The Cambridge handbook of thinking and reasoning* (pp. 775–802). New York: Cambridge University Press.

Rogers, C. R. (1983). *Freedom to Learn for the 80's*. Columbus, OH: Merrill.

Schore, A. (1994). *Affect regulation*. Hillsdale, NJ: Erlbaum.

Schore, A. N. (2001). The effects of early relational trauma on right brain development, affect regulation, and infant mental health. *Infant Mental Health Journal*, 22, 201–269.

Shonkoff, J. P., & Phillips, D. A. (2000). *From neurons to neighborhoods: The science of early childhood development*. Washington, DC: National Academy Press.

Siegel, D. J. (1999). *The developing mind: How relationships and the brain interact to shape who we are*. New York: Guilford Press.

Solnit, R. (2009). *A paradise built in hell: The extraordinary communities that arise in disaster*. New York: Viking.

Stam, R., Akkermans, L. M., & Wiegant, V. M. (1997). Trauma and the gut: Interactions between stressful experience and intestinal function. *Gut, 40,* 704–709.
Sternberg, R. (1998). Abilities are forms of developing expertise. *Educational Researcher, 3,* 22–35.
Sternberg, R. J. (1999). Intelligence as developing expertise. *Contemporary Educational Psychology, 24*(4), 359–375.
Thompson, R. (2009). Early foundations: Conscience and the development of moral character. In D. Narvaez & D. K. Lapsley (Eds.), *Moral personality, identity and character: An interdisciplinary future* (pp. 159–184). New York: Cambridge University Press.
Tronick, E. (2007). *The neurobehavioral and social-emotional development of infants and children.* New York: W.W. Norton.
Trout, J.D. (2009). *The empathy gap.* NewYork: Viking/Penguin.
Urdan, T., & Midgley, C. (2001). Academic self-handicapping: What we know; What more there is to learn. *Educational Psychology Review, 13,* 115–138.
Urdan, T., Midgley, C., & Anderman, E. (1998). The role of classroom goal structure in students use of self-handicapping strategies. *American Educational Research Journal, 35,* 101–122.
Urmson, J. O. (1988). *Aristotle's ethics.* Oxford: Blackwell.
U.S. Department of Health and Human Services, Substance Abuse and Mental Health Services Administration. (1999). *Mental health: A report of the surgeon general.* Rockville, MD: Center for Mental Health Services, National Institutes of Health, National Institute of Mental Health.
Varela, F. (1999). *Ethical know-how: Action, wisdom, and cognition.* Stanford CA: Stanford University Press.
Varela, F. J., Thompson, E., & Rosch, E. (1991). *The embodied mind: Cognitive science and* human experience. Cambridge, MA: MIT Press.
Vaydich, J., Khmelkov, V., & Narvaez, D. (April, 2007). *Comparing middle school learning motivations with ethical attitudes and behaviors.* Chicago: American Educational Research Association.
Walker, L. J., & Frimer, J. (2009). Moral personality exemplified. In D. Narvaez & D. K. Lapsley (Eds.), *Moral personality, identity and character: An interdisciplinary future* (pp. 232–255). New York: Cambridge University Press.
Watson, M., & Eckert, L. (2003). *Learning to trust.* San Francisco: Jossey-Bass.
Weaver, I. C., Szyf, M., & Meaney, M. J. (2002). From maternal care to gene expression: DNA methylation and the maternal programming of stress responses. *Endocrine Research, 28,* 699.
Zeedyk, M. S. (2008). *What's life in a baby buggy like?: The impact of buggy orientation on parent–infant interaction and infant stress.* London: National Literacy Trust. Retrieved November 21, 2008, from http://www.literacytrust.org.uk/
Zuckerman, B., Bauchner, H., Parker, S., & Cabral, H. (1990). Maternal depressive symptoms during pregnancy, and newborn irritability. *Journal of Developmental & Behavioral Pediatrics. 11*(4), 190–194.

DARCIA NARVAEZ is an associate professor of psychology at the University of Notre Dame. She is director of the Collaborative for Ethical Education at the University of Notre Dame. E-mail: dnarvaez@nd.edu, Web page: http://www.nd.edu/~dnarvaez/

INDEX

Other Titles Available in the New Directions for Child and Adolescent Development Series

Reed W. Larson and Lene Arnett Jensen, Editors-in-Chief
William Damon, Founding Editor-in-Chief

For a complete list of back issues, please visit www.josseybass.com/go/ndcad

CAD128 ***Focus on Gender: Parent and Child Contributions to the Socialization of Emotional Competence***
Amy Kennedy Root, Susanne A. Denham, Editors
Gender's influence on human development is all encompassing. In fact, "Virtually all of human functioning has a gendered cast—appearance, mannerisms, communication, temperament, activities at home and outside, aspirations, and values" (Ruble, Martin, & Berenbaum, 2006, p. 858).

In short, gender impacts growth in a multitude of developmental domains, including the development of emotion and emotional competence. Although emotions are, in part, biological, the meanings of emotions and appropriateness of emotional expression are socialized. In the early years of life, socialization primarily takes place via interactions within the family, and characteristics of both parents and children may affect the process of emotion socialization. Gender is one critically important moderator of what and how children learn about emotion because culture determines the appropriateness of emotional displays for males and females.

The goal of this sourcebook is to provide a comprehensive volume addressing what we see as the critical issues in the study of gender, emotion socialization, and the development of emotional competence. Each of the chapters provides evidence for the pervasive role that gender plays in emotional development and provides a framework to better understand the development of emotion in boys and girls.
ISBN 978-04706-47868

CAD127 ***Social Anxiety in Childhood: Bridging Developmental and Clinical Perspectives***
Heidi Gazelle, Kenneth H. Rubin, Editors
Social anxiety in childhood is the focus of research in three psychological research traditions: developmental studies emphasizing dispositional constructs such as behavioral inhibition and its biological substrates; developmental investigations emphasizing affective-behavioral characteristics (anxious solitude/withdrawal) and their parent–child and peerrelational precursors and moderators; and clinical investigations of social anxiety disorder (also known as social phobia) emphasizing a variety of etiological factors, diagnosis, and treatment. In this volume, we review and identify gaps in extant evidence that permit (or impede) researchers from the three traditions to translate their core definitional constructs in ways that would facilitate the use of one another's research. Intimately connected to this translation of constructs is a discussion of the conceptualization of core states (anxiety, wariness, solitude) and their manifestations across childhood, as well as corresponding methodologies. Extant research is analyzed from an integrative, overarching framework of developmental psychopathology in which children's adjustment is conceptualized as multiply determined such that children who share certain risks may display diverse adjustment over time (multifinality) and children with diverse risks may develop shared adaptational difficulties over time (equifinality). Finally, key themes for future

integrative research are identified and implications for preventative and early intervention in childhood social anxiety are discussed.
ISBN 978-04706-18059

CAD126 ***Siblings as Agents of Socialization***
Laurie Kramer, Katherine J. Conger, Editors
Siblings have considerable influence on children's development, yet most human development research has neglected the investigation of sibling socialization in favor of a focus on parental socialization. This volume uses a family systems framework to examine the ways in which siblings contribute uniquely to one another's social and emotional development. The groundbreaking lines of research in this volume address mechanisms by which children are influenced by their sisters and brothers, ways in which these processes of sibling socialization are similar to and different from those with parents, and conditions under which sibling socialization has positive versus negative impact on individual development. Throughout this volume, attention is devoted to contextual factors that moderate sibling influences, such as family structure, life course events, ethnicity and culture, gender, and demographic indicators.
ISBN 978-04706-14594

CAD125 ***Evidentiality: A Window Into Language and Cognitive Development***
Stanka A. Fitneva, Tomoko Matsui, Editors
Much recent research investigates children's understanding of the sources of human knowledge and the relation of this understanding to socio-cognitive development. This volume of *New Directions for Child and Adolescent Development* highlights new research in this area that focuses on evidentials: word affixes and sentence particles that indicate the speaker's source of knowledge—for example, perception, inference, or hearsay. Evidentials are a feature of about a quarter of the languages in the world and have a variety of interesting characteristics. For example, in contrast to lexical alternatives familiar from English, such as "I saw," they are extremely frequent. The volume brings together scholars pioneering research on evidentiality in Bulgarian, Japanese, Tibetan, and Turkish. Their contributions to this volume provide a glimpse at the diversity of evidential systems around the globe while examining a number of provocative questions: How do evidentials mediate children's acquisition of knowledge from others' testimony? What is the relation between grammaticalized and lexical expressions of source of knowledge? Does the acquisition of an evidential system boost source monitoring and inferential skills? The volume is a compelling illustration of the relevance of evidentiality to broadening our understanding of development in many domains, including theory of mind, memory, and knowledge acquisition.
ISBN 978-04705-69658

CAD124 ***Coping and the Development of Regulation***
Ellen A. Skinner, Melanie J. Zimmer-Gembeck, Editors
A developmental conceptualization that emphasizes coping as regulation under stress opens the way to explore synergies between coping and regulatory processes, including self-regulation; behavioral, emotion, attention, and action regulation; ego control; self-control; compliance; and volition. This volume, with chapters written by experts on the development of regulation and coping during childhood and adolescence, is the first to explore these synergies. The volume is geared toward researchers working in the broad areas of regulation, coping, stress, adversity, and resilience. For regulation researchers, it offers opportunities to focus on age-graded changes in how these processes function under stress and to consider multiple targets of

regulation simultaneously—emotion, attention, behavior—that typically are examined in isolation. For researchers interested in coping, this volume offers invigorating theoretical and operational ideas. For researchers studying stress, adversity, and resilience, the volume highlights coping as one pathway through which exposure to adversity shapes children's long-term development. The authors also address cross-cutting developmental themes, such as the role of stress, coping, and social relationships in the successive integration of regulatory subsystems, the emergence of autonomous regulation, and the progressive construction of the kinds of regulatory resources and routines that allow flexible constructive coping under successively higher levels of stress and adversity. All chapters emphasize the importance of integrative multilevel perspectives in bringing together work on the neurobiology of stress, temperament, attachment, regulation, personal resources, relationships, stress exposure, and social contexts in studying processes of coping, adversity, and resilience.
ISBN 978-04705-31372

CAD 123 **Social Interaction and the Development of Executive Function**
Charlie Lewis, Jeremy I. M. Carpendale, Editors
Executive function consists of higher cognitive skills that are involved in the control of thought, action, and emotion. It has been linked to neural systems involving the prefrontal cortex, but a full definition of the term has remained elusive partly because it includes such a complex set of cognitive processes. Relatively little is known about the processes that promote development of executive function, and how it is linked to children's social behavior. The key factor examined by the chapters in this issue is the role of social interaction, and the chapters take an increasingly broad perspective. Two end pieces introduce the topic as a whole (Chapter 1) and present an integrative commentary on the articles (Chapter 6) in an attempt to stress the social origins of executive function, in contrast to many contemporary cognitive approaches. The empirical contributions in between examine the roles of parental scaffolding of young preschoolers (Chapter 2), the links between maternal education and conversational support (Chapter 3), how such family background factors and social skills extend into adolescence (Chapter 4), and wider cultural influences (Chapter 5) on development of executive skills. This volume is aimed at a broad range of developmental researchers and practitioners interested in the influences of family background and interactions as well as educational and cultural processes on development of the child's self-control and social understanding. Such relationships have wide implications for many aspects of the lives of children and adolescents.
ISBN 978-04704-89017

CAD 122 **Core Competencies to Prevent Problem Behaviors and Promote Positive Youth Development**
Nancy G. Guerra, Catherine P. Bradshaw, Editors
Adolescence generally is considered a time of experimentation and increased involvement in risk or problem behaviors, including early school leaving, violence, substance use, and high-risk sexual behavior. In this volume, the authors show how individual competencies linked to well-being can reduce youth involvement in these risk behaviors. Five core competencies are emphasized: a positive sense of self, self-control, decision-making skills, a moral system of belief, and prosocial connectedness. A central premise of this volume is that high levels of the core competencies provide a marker for positive youth development, whereas low levels increase the likelihood of adolescent risk behavior. The authors summarize the empirical literature linking these competencies to each risk behavior, providing examples from

developmental and prevention research. They highlight programs and policies in the United States and internationally that have changed one or more dimensions of the core competencies through efforts designed to build individual skills, strengthen relationships, and enhance opportunities and supports across multiple developmental contexts.
ISBN 978-04704-42166

CAD 121 ***Beyond the Family: Contexts of Immigrant Children's Development***
Hirokazu Yoshikawa, Niobe Way, Editors
Immigration in the United States has become a central focus of policy and public concern in the first decade of the 21st century. This volume aims to broaden developmental research on children and youth in immigrant families. Much of the research on immigrant children and youth concentrates on family characteristics such as parenting, demographic, or human capital features. In this volume, we consider the developmental consequences for immigrant youth of broader contexts such as social networks, peer discrimination in school and out-of-school settings, legal contexts, and access to institutional resources. Chapters answer questions such as: How do experiences of discrimination affect the lives of immigrant youth? How do social networks of immigrant families influence children's learning? How do immigrant parents' citizenship status influence family life and their children's development? In examining factors as disparate as discrimination based on physical appearance, informal adult helpers, and access to drivers' licenses, these chapters serve to enrich our notions of how culture and context shape human development, as well as inform practice and public policy affecting immigrant families.
ISBN 978-04704-17300

CAD 120 ***The Intersections of Personal and Social Identities***
Margarita Azmitia, Moin Syed, Kimberley Radmacher, Editors
This volume brings together an interdisciplinary set of social scientists who are pioneering ways to research and theorize the connections between personal and social identity development in children, adolescents, and emerging adults. The authors of the seven chapters address the volume's three goals: (1) illustrating how theory and research in identity develop-ment are enriched by an interdisciplinary approach, (2) providing a rich developmental picture of personal and social identity development, and (3) examining the connections among multiple identities. Several chapters provide practical suggestions for individuals, agencies, and schools and universities that work with children, adolescents, and emerging adults in diverse communities across the United States.
ISBN 978-04703-72838

CAD 119 ***Social Class and Transitions to Adulthood***
Jeylan T. Mortimer, Editor
This volume of *New Directions for Child and Adolescent Development* is inspired by a stirring address that Frank Furstenberg delivered at the 2006 Meeting of the Society for Research on Adolescence, "Diverging Development: The Not So Invisible Hand of Social Class in the United States." He called on social scientists interested in the study of development to expand their purview beyond investigations of the developmental impacts of poverty and consider the full gamut of social class variation in our increasingly unequal society. The gradations of class alter the social supports, resources, and opportunities, as well as the constraints, facing parents as they attempt to guide their children toward the acquisition of adult roles. This volume examines the impacts of social class origin on the highly formative period of transition to

adulthood. Drawing on findings from the Youth Development Study and other sources, the authors examine social class differences in adult child–parent relationships, intimacy and family formation, attainment of higher education, the school-to-work transition, the emergence of work-family conflict, and harassment in the workplace. The authors indicate new directions for research that will contribute to understanding the problems facing young people today. These chapters will persuade those making social policy to develop social interventions that will level the playing field and increase the opportunities for disadvantaged youth to become healthy and productive adults.
ISBN 978-04702-93621

CAD 118 ***Social Network Analysis and Children's Peer Relationships***
Philip C. Rodkin, Laura D. Hanish, Editors
Social network analysis makes it possible to determine how large and dense children's peer networks are, how central children are within their networks, the various structural configurations that characterize social groups, and which peers make up individual children's networks. By centering the child within his or her social system, it is possible to understand the socialization processes that draw children toward or away from particular peers, as well as those who contribute to peer influence. This volume of *New Directions for Child and Adolescent Development* demonstrates how social network analysis provides insights into the ways in which peer groups contribute to children's and adolescents' development—from gender and intergroup relations, to aggression and bullying, to academic achievement. Together the chapters in this volume depict the complex, nested, and dynamic structure of peer groups and explain how social structure defines developmental processes.
ISBN 978-04702-59665

CAD 117 ***Attachment in Adolescence: Reflections and New Angles***
Miri Scharf, Ofra Mayseless, Editors
In recent years, the number of empirical studies examining attachment in adolescence has grown considerably, with most focusing on individual differences in attachment security. This volume goes a step further in extending our knowledge and understanding. The physical, cognitive, emotional, and social changes that characterize adolescence invite a closer conceptual look at attachment processes and organization during this period. The chapter authors, leading researchers in attachment in adolescence, address key topics in attachment processes in adolescence. These include issues such as the normative distancing from parents and the growing importance of peers, the formation of varied attachment hierarchies, the changing nature of attachment dynamics from issues of survival to issues of affect regulation, siblings' similarity in attachment representations, individual differences in social information processes in adolescence, and stability and change in attachment representations in a risk sample. Together the chapters provide a compelling discussion of intriguing issues and broaden our understanding of attachment in adolescence and the basic tenets of attachment theory at large.
ISBN 978-04702-25608

CAD 116 ***Linking Parents and Family to Adolescent Peer Relations: Ethnic and Cultural Considerations***
B. Bradford Brown, Nina S. Mounts, Editors
Ethnic and cultural background shapes young people's development and behavior in a variety of ways, including their interactions with family and peers. The intersection of family and peer worlds during childhood has been studied extensively, but only recently has this work been extended to adolescence. This volume of *New Directions for Child and Adolescent Development*

highlights new research linking family to adolescent peer relations from a multiethnic perspective. Using qualitative and quantitative research methods, the contributors consider similarities and differences within and between ethnic groups in regard to several issues: parents' goals and strategies for guiding young people to adaptive peer relationships, how peer relationships shape and are shaped by kin relationships, and the specific strategies that adolescents and parents use to manage information about peers or negotiate rules about peer interactions and relationships. Findings emphasize the central role played by sociocultural context in shaping the complex, bidirectional processes that link family members to adolescents' peer social experiences.
ISBN 978-04701-78010

CAD 115 ***Conventionality in Cognitive Development: How Children Acquire Shared Representations in Language, Thought, and Action***
Chuck W. Kalish, Mark A. Sabbagh, Editors
An important part of cognitive development is coming to think in culturally normative ways. Children learn the right names for objects, proper functions for tools, appropriate ways to categorize, and the rules for games. In each of these cases, what makes a given practice normative is not naturally given. There is not necessarily any objectively better or worse way to do any of these things. Instead, what makes them correct is that people agree on how they should be done, and each of these practices therefore has an important conventional basis. The chapters in this volume highlight the fact that successful participation in practices of language, cognition, and play depends on children's ability to acquire representations that other members of their social worlds share. Each of these domains poses problems of identifying normative standards and achieving coordination across agents. This volume brings together scholars from diverse areas in cognitive development to consider the psychological mechanisms supporting the use and acquisition of conventional knowledge.
ISBN 978-07879-96970

CAD 114 ***Respect and Disrespect: Cultural and Developmental Origins***
David W. Schwalb, Barbara J. Schwalb, Editors
Respect enables children and teenagers to value other people, institutions, traditions, and themselves. Disrespect is the agent that dissolves positive relationships and fosters hostile and cynical relationships. Unfortunately, parents, educators, children, and adolescents in many societies note with alarm a growing problem of disrespect and a decline in respect for self and others. Is this disturbing trend a worldwide problem? To answer this question, we must begin to study the developmental and cultural origins of respect and disrespect. Five research teams report that respect and disrespect are influenced by experiences in the family, school, community, and, most importantly, the broader cultural setting. The chapters introduce a new topic area for mainstream developmental sciences that is relevant to the interests of scholars, educators, practitioners, and policymakers.
ISBN 978-07879-95584

CAD 113 ***The Modernization of Youth Transitions in Europe***
Manuela du Bois-Reymond, Lynne Chisholm, Editors
This compelling volume focuses on what it is like to be young in the rapidly changing, enormously diverse world region that is early 21st century Europe. Designed for a North American readership interested in youth and young adulthood, *The Modernization of Youth Transitions in Europe* provides a rich fund of theoretical insight and empirical evidence about the implications of contemporary modernization processes for young people living, learning, and working across Europe. Chapters have been specially written for this volume

by well-known youth sociologists; they cover a wide range of themes against a shared background of the reshaping of the life course and its constituent phases toward greater openness and contigency. New modes of learning accompany complex routes into employment and career under rapidly changing labor market conditions and occupational profiles, while at the same time new family and lifestyle forms are developing alongside greater intergenerational responsibilities in the face of the retreat of the modern welfare state. The complex patterns of change for today's young Europeans are set into a broader framework that analyzes the emergence and character of European youth research and youth policy in recent years.
ISBN 978-07879-88890

CAD 112 ***Rethinking Positive Adolescent Female Sexual Development***
Lisa M. Diamond, Editor
This volume provides thoughtful and diverse perspectives on female adolescent sexuality. These perspectives integrate biological, cultural, and interpersonal influences on adolescent girls' sexuality, and highlight the importance of using multiple methods to investigate sexual ideation and experience. Traditional portrayals cast adolescent females as sexual gatekeepers whose primary task is to fend off boys' sexual overtures and set aside their own sexual desires in order to reduce their risks for pregnancy and sexually transmitted diseases. Yet an increasing number of thoughtful and constructive critiques have challenged this perspective, arguing for more sensitive, in-depth, multimethod investigations into the positive meanings of sexuality for adolescent girls that will allow us to conceptualize (and, ideally, advocate for) healthy sexual-developmental trajectories. Collectively, authors of this volume take up this movement and chart exciting new directions for the next generation of developmental research on adolescent female sexuality.
ISBN 978-07879-87350

CAD 111 ***Family Mealtime as a Context for Development and Socialization***
Reed W. Larson, Angela R. Wiley, Kathryn R. Branscomb, Editors
This issue examines the impact of family mealtime on the psychological development of young people. In the popular media, family mealtime is often presented as a vital institution for the socialization and development of young people, but also as one that is "going the way of the dinosaur." Although elements such as fast food and TV have become a part of many family mealtimes, evidence is beginning to suggest that mealtimes can also provide rich opportunities for children's and adolescents' development. While what happens at mealtimes varies greatly among families, an outline of the forms and functions of mealtimes is beginning to emerge from this research. In this issue, leading mealtime researchers from the fields of history, cultural anthropology, psycholinguistics, psychology, and nutrition critically review findings from each of their disciplines, giving primary focus on family mealtimes in the United States. The authors in this issue examine the history of family mealtimes, describe contemporary mealtime practices, elucidate the differing transactional processes that occur, and evaluate evidence on the outcomes associated with family mealtimes from children and adolescents.
ISBN 978-07879-85776

NEW DIRECTIONS FO 

NT DEVELOPMENT

ORDER F N AND SINGLE ISSUES

DISCOUNTED BACK ISSUES:

Use this form to receive 20% off all back issues of *New Directions for Child and Adolescent Development.* All single issues priced at **$23.20** (normally $29.00)

TITLE	ISSUE NO.	ISBN

Call 888-378-2537 or see mailing instructions below. When calling, mention the promotional code JBNND to receive your discount. For a complete list of issues, please visit www.josseybass.com/go/ndcad

SUBSCRIPTIONS: (1 YEAR, 4 ISSUES)

☐ New Order ☐ Renewal

U.S.	☐ Individual: $89	☐ Institutional: $315
Canada/Mexico	☐ Individual: $89	☐ Institutional: $355
All Others	☐ Individual: $113	☐ Institutional: $389

Call 888-378-2537 or see mailing and pricing instructions below.
Online subscriptions are available at www.onlinelibrary.wiley.com

ORDER TOTALS:

Issue / Subscription Amount: $ ____________

Shipping Amount: $ ____________
(for single issues only – subscription prices include shipping)

Total Amount: $ ____________

SHIPPING CHARGES:	
First Item	$5.00
Each Add'l Item	$3.00

(No sales tax for U.S. subscriptions. Canadian residents, add GST for subscription orders. Individual rate subscriptions must be paid by personal check or credit card. Individual rate subscriptions may not be resold as library copies.)

BILLING & SHIPPING INFORMATION:

☐ **PAYMENT ENCLOSED:** *(U.S. check or money order only. All payments must be in U.S. dollars.)*

☐ **CREDIT CARD:** ☐ VISA ☐ MC ☐ AMEX

Card number ____________ Exp. Date ____________

Card Holder Name ____________ Card Issue # ____________

Signature ____________ Day Phone ____________

☐ **BILL ME:** *(U.S. institutional orders only. Purchase order required.)*

Purchase order # ____________
Federal Tax ID 13559302 • GST 89102-8052

Name ____________

Address ____________

Phone ____________ E-mail ____________

Copy or detach page and send to: **John Wiley & Sons, PTSC, 5th Floor 989 Market Street, San Francisco, CA 94103-1741**

Order Form can also be faxed to: **888-481-2665**

PROMO JBNND